HAYEK

VS

KEYNES

HAYEK
VS
KEYNES
A Battle of Ideas

Thomas Hoerber

REAKTION BOOKS

Published by
Reaktion Books Ltd
Unit 32, Waterside
44–48 Wharf Road
London N1 7UX, UK
www.reaktionbooks.co.uk

First published 2017
First published in paperback 2025
Copyright © Thomas Hoerber 2017

Printed and bound in Great Britain
by CPI Group (UK) Ltd, Croydon CR0 4YY

A catalogue record for this book is available from the British Library

ISBN 978 1 83639 033 6

Contents

Introduction *7*

1 From the Eighteenth to the Twentieth Century:
Momentous Change and Stable Elements *17*

2 Hayek's Road to Liberty *26*

3 Information and Planning *36*

4 Keynes's General Theory *43*

5 Man is *Not* the Master of His Own Fate:
Misguided Socialist Idealism *56*

6 Liberal Polemic, or, the Threat of
National Socialism *70*

7 The Necessity of Planning *77*

8 Liberty and Totalitarianism *88*

9 International Organizations and
European Integration *102*

Conclusion *118*

Abbreviations *131*
References *133*
Bibliography *147*
Acknowledgements *155*
Index *157*

Introduction

A t its best, economic theory really tries to explain how society works, or how it should work. This in turn comes very close to what political theory does. Both find their zenith in great works such as those by Adam Smith or Karl Marx, which have become the embodiment of social theory. Naturally, Marx and Smith were not the first to write about the inner workings of society, and they were certainly not the last. In the tradition of the history of political and economic thought, the present book traces this historical line of social sciences to more contemporary disciples, namely Friedrich von Hayek (1899–1992) and John Maynard Keynes (1883–1946), whose writings have also been elevated to classics. The development of ideas clearly takes time, and that goes for the understanding of economic and political theory developed by those great economic thinkers as well.

This book is not about economics, but rather about the history of economic thought. The purpose of the following analysis is to get an idea of the current relevance of their two major studies as economic theories. In our time of globalization, are the theories outdated works, which we can safely leave slumbering on the shelf? Or are there still lessons to be learned from these theories that can be applied to the current economic problems of our society today? This book will set out the merits and the deficiencies of both Hayek's and Keynes's concepts, because they continue to be the most important archetypes of economic theory, and eventually lead to the question of the role of economic theory in our society. Economic modelling and the mathematical abstraction of economic realities have replaced economic narratives of the type Marx or Smith wrote. Hayek and Keynes foreshadowed that development. This book tries to do the opposite. It tells the story of how Hayek and Keynes conceived the proper workings of society through economics. Economic theory is seen as a theory of society setting norms and objectives to which an ideal society should aspire to. For Hayek that would be freedom in all its forms; for Keynes that would be full employment, but not only that. We will see whether economic theory can still fulfil that normative function today and, if not, whether it would then be useful to develop such a strand of normative economics in the present time.

The background to the writing of two of the seminal works of economic theory in the twentieth century was tragedy: the Great Depression of the 1930s and its devastating economic consequence, the Second World War. The question of what can we learn from the past for a better future has always been considered problematic by historians. What is certain is that the Great Depression brought Keynes and Hayek to develop their economic theories against the backdrop of its most striking consequences. Hayek would argue that making profit and engaging in economic activity in itself served the moral cause of maintaining society, because it would create wealth that would then naturally be spread out among the entrepreneurs and the workers; in short, among all active citizens of a society. For Keynes, it showed the errors in liberal market logic, which he called the 'classical theory'. For him, the Great Depression was proof that the simple drive to make profit and the resulting liberal economic equation of supply and demand did not serve the benefit of all society. It was the unacceptable degree of unemployment, caused by the faltering of trade and thus of industrial growth across the developed world, which led Keynes to write his *General Theory of Employment, Interest and Money*, published in 1936.[1] The need to avoid the mass unemployment caused by a malfunctioning of this very market logic became the moral core of Keynes's theory.

In contrast, Hayek saw the planning of the economic framework – which Keynes so strongly advocated – as the 'thin end of the wedge', the beginning of the end to freedom in all its forms. His key work, *The Road to Serfdom* (1944), was written during the height of the Second World War. Its background was the growing realization that crimes against humanity were being committed on an appalling scale in the heart of a continent once proud of its civility. If what later came to be known as the Holocaust was certainly the worst example of these crimes, the Nazi leaders also presided over and promoted the wholesale corruption of long-entrenched values of decency, common sense and non-violence. The German people, once admired as a great *Kulturvolk*, became – seemingly – an amorphous mass of mindless but highly organized savages, spreading death and wholesale destruction throughout Europe. Worse, perhaps, Hayek feared that one effect of the war could be to strengthen those forces in Britain which had helped to prepare the ground for the Nazis in Germany.[2] This is the context, and at the same time the reason, for Hayek writing his *Road to Serfdom*, with which he became the banner bearer of liberalism in the twentieth century. It is he who throws down the gauntlet to his main rival, Keynes. Here a battle of ideas – essentially, central planning versus the free market – began, which inspired both Hayek and Keynes to elaborate ideologies that became and have remained extremely influential.

This book is an attempt to show the importance of Hayek's work on liberalism, which he called 'the abandoned road'. It is true that his work has become, with time, the basis for the currently dominant neoliberal ideology. However, the original purpose of *The Road to Serfdom* was to show the perversions in Nazi Germany as the backdrop against which liberalism was more necessary than ever. In the post-war period, this would lead to the development of totalitarianism as a criterion of fascist and communist dictatorships, which defined the Cold War period. In comparison with his liberal forebears, such as Adam Smith, J. S. Mill or Edmund Burke, Hayek was more moderate, and readily conceded that there were limits to freedom where such freedom clearly contradicted the common interest or civilized levels of decency. A good example is child labour, which in classical liberal theory was often seen as a normal market resource.[3] Smith ignored it mostly.[4] And left-leaning economic theory considered it manifestly wrong.[5] After the Second World War, Hayek also thought that international organizations could well help to curb the depredations of raptor capitalism, whose only objective was profit, regardless of the consequences. In the two examples of child labour and international organizations, we can already discern a softening of attitudes, which led among other changes to the foundation of the Bretton Woods institutions, which have tried to make international politics more docile in the post-war period. Keynes was of course closely involved in their creation. And this commitment to world institutions, such as the United Nations, is an important link between Hayek and Keynes. At the same time, these international institutions are an important hallmark of the post-war period, and indeed were a lesson from the Second World War. They were set up with the aim of avoiding another world war. Of course there were predecessors, such as the League of Nations, but up to now post-war international institutions have been more powerful and more successful. Eventually, setting up such institutions limited the freedom of action of states and individuals. For states, this was meant to curtail the profit rationale behind arms manufacturing, which was often a reason for making war at the time. This led to the not-so-liberal question of how much freedom for making profit is good for society as a whole – a question which this book will try to address, although almost certainly with only limited success, because the moral judgement on which the answer is based is always an individual one. On that individual level today, the question must therefore also be posed: how much profit is each of us looking for? How much profit can one legitimately aspire to make from investments? And where does greed start? Adam Smith and later Chicago economists in neoliberalism argued for profit maximization.[6] We will see that Hayek's liberalism goes far beyond that. Today, in the age of globalization these questions have more relevance than ever, because sustainable growth has to be achieved with the corresponding economic patterns and moral behaviour in global concert.

Keynes defended fundamental freedoms in his *General Theory* just as vigorously, arguing that moderate planning was necessary to safeguard political liberty, a task at which the interwar laissez-faire economy – based on what Keynes calls the 'classical economic theory' – had conspicuously failed. In contrast with the *General Theory*, which is a detailed and often densely mathematical development of an economic theory, Hayek's *Road to Serfdom* is a relentless indictment of the wrongs of his time. Hayek saw the root cause of the Second World War in wrong economic decisions taken by democratic regimes in the 1920s and '30s – notably by the Weimar Republic, the first democracy in Germany. Resulting mass unemployment, hyperinflation and eventually the breakdown of democracy led to the rise of Hitler. These mistakes led eventually to the loss of all freedoms in the dictatorships of the 1930s and '40s. Mussolini and Hitler were the original villains from the perspective of liberal Western democracies; Stalin was added to that list soon after the Allied victory in the Second World War. From his analysis of the mistakes of Western liberal democracies before the Second World War, Hayek deduced an economic theory based on 'classical liberalism', which makes the case for a reinvigoration of liberalism. Starting from how society was and how it should be, Hayek deduced that classical liberal values would be the best way to guarantee a good society. Hayek then followed up with his own adaptation of liberalism (of which more later).

In contrast to Hayek, Keynes clearly preferred an inductive method, meaning he went in his reasoning from small examples to general rules.[7] His objective, too, was the economic well-being of citizens. A regular income for everyone followed from that. Only full employment could guarantee it. For Keynes, the design of a just economic system would have to reflect that objective. This had been the political rationale behind Franklin D. Roosevelt's New Deal policy. Economic planning had become the dominant economic theory of the late 1930s in the U.S. Later, the war effort added another reason for economic planning, not just in the U.S. but in Britain – Hayek's main concern – and indeed across the Western democracies. Keynes's *General Theory* gave theoretical legitimacy to these policies, though it did not necessarily contribute to their initial inception.

The interesting point here is that classical liberal theory was the dominant theory, which Keynes had convincingly challenged in the mid-1930s through his *General Theory*. When Hayek was defending liberalism in the early 1940s, he saw himself in the role of the underdog, on the defensive. In his *Road to Serfdom* he provided an economic narrative, which was the opposite of making economics more objective, in the manner of the natural sciences. He had demanded more objectivity for the discipline of economics in his seminal article of 'Economics and Knowledge'.[8] Keynes actually did it, or at least he claimed to be making economics more theoretical. Both men – Hayek in his earlier work and Keynes in his *General Theory* – tried to arrive at more objectivity, as every good researcher does. Keynes states clearly in the introduction to his *General Theory* that 'its main purpose is to deal with difficult questions of theory, and only in the second place with the applications of this theory to practice.'[9] With that, Keynes claimed the moral high ground in the intradisciplinary contest. He was supported by the general political trend of economic planning at the time. Moreover, Hayek's inconsistency in demanding more logic while delivering an economic narrative in *The Road to Serfdom* meant that Hayek's overall argument was considered wanting in the 1940s and well into the post-war period.

Such lack of appreciation was a theme that resurfaced several times during Hayek's academic career. Keynes, in contrast, seemed very relaxed about criticism of his work: 'Those who are strongly wedded to what I shall call "the classical theory", will fluctuate, I expect, between a belief that I am quite wrong and a belief that I am saying nothing new.'[10] One may call this Cambridge arrogance, or, alternatively, an enlightened perception of Keynes's academic environment. It certainly shows confidence, merited or not, in his work, which one finds less with Hayek. In any case, classical (liberal) theory, the dominant approach up to the early 1930s, was superseded by Keynes's *General Theory*. Keynes, referring to Marx, clarifies this further, by naming classical liberal economists such as

> [David] Ricardo and James Mill and their *predecessors*, that is to say for the founders of the theory which culminated in the Ricardian economics. I have become accustomed, perhaps perpetrating a solecism, to include in 'the classical school' the *followers* of Ricardo, those, that is to say, who adopted and perfected the theory of the Ricardian economics, including (for example) J. S. Mill, Marshall, Edgeworth and Prof. Pigou.[11]

Beyond their opposing economic arguments and methodologies, Hayek and Keynes were also opposed in their views on the destination of economics as a discipline. Despite the fact that Keynes uses more formulae and mathematics in his *General Theory* than Hayek does in his *Road to Serfdom*, Keynes urges those interested in his work not to get lost in the formalization of economics:

> Too large a proportion of recent 'mathematical' economics are [*sic*] mere concoctions, as imprecise as the initial assumptions they rest on, which allow the author to lose sight of the complexities and interdependencies of the real world in a maze of pretentious and unhelpful symbols.[12]

Keynes goes even further in his 'generalized [mathematical] statement of the Quantity Theory of Money' when he says that mathematics does not necessarily bring more clarity than a good narrative:

> I do not myself attach much value to manipulations of this kind; and I would repeat the warning, which I have given above, that they involve just as much tacit assumption as to what variables are taken as independent ... as does ordinary discourse, whilst I doubt if they carry us any further than ordinary discourse can.[13]

The appeal for more trust in economic narratives and in qualitative analysis in general will be another theme of this book. Today, economics has become overwhelmingly quantitative. Relying solely on Keynes and Hayek narratives about the history and the economics of their time, this book will try to show that qualitative economics can still provide a meaningful analysis of current economies, and perhaps even of society as a whole. Modern economics has lost not only the capacity, but even the aspiration to do that.

In his earlier work, for example the essay on 'Economics and Knowledge' (1937), Hayek seems to go in the opposite direction. He demanded more objectivity through the introduction of logic and mathematics into the discipline of economics.

> My criticism of recent tendencies to make economic theory more and more formal is not that they have gone too far, but that they have not yet been carried far enough to complete the isolation of this branch of logic and to restore to its rightful place the investigation of causal processes, using formal economic theory as a tool in the same way as mathematics.[14]

Interestingly enough, *The Road to Serfdom* does not reflect at all this tendency to formalization in economics; rather the opposite, in that it provides a very lucid narrative of the merits of liberalism. The present book will go in the same direction.

This leads to a major consideration of this book: the question as to the direction of economics. Economic theory in particular has become more and more formalized through the extensive application of mathematical modelling. This tendency has taken the discipline away from the purpose of classical economics, in which such theories sought to explain the functioning of society as a whole and the role the economy should play in it. Recent economic theory – more recent than Hayek's and Keynes's – seems to have lost this explanatory potential and, not least, accessibility for laypeople who cannot or do not want to struggle with economic models. The question to be asked, then, is whether economics should content itself with such formal models of the economy, letting the non-experts fall by the wayside. The alternative would be for economics to find its way back to its roots, of providing a narrative of the workings of the economy in society, which any interested reader can understand.

It should also be stated here in this Introduction that this book will not deal with the enormous amount of secondary literature which has been written on both Hayek's and Keynes's work, although it will use some selected works where they are interesting and relevant for the understanding of the key arguments of either figure. A good example is the work of Theodore Burczak, who has adapted Hayek's economics beyond the somewhat artificial debate of the 1930s and '40s. Burczak helped turn the originally opposing doctrines of Keynesian planning and Hayek's free market liberalism into a 'fruitful dialogue' which eventually asks questions regarding the societal relevance of economic theory beyond the limits of economics as a discipline – which has become rather difficult to access for anyone who is not an expert in economic modelling and applied economic mathematics.[15] Despite the use of some secondary literature such as this, the main analytical focus will remain on *The Road to Serfdom* and the *General Theory*. The reason for this limitation is simple: this book is an attempt to get to the root of the two economic theories, deliberately disregarding later interpretations, which are not necessarily seen as distortions, but by definition are less relevant than the original works. This conviction comes from the historical approach the current book will be taking. Historical research in this sense focuses principally on primary sources and uses secondary sources only as support, where necessary, for the interpretation of primary sources.

This book will point to the European Union (EU) as one element of hope. Since 1950 it has been a thriving association of nation states which may well provide the only existing framework powerful enough, but at the same time sufficiently flexible, to allow its members to prosper without harming the rest of the world. The EU can pass binding laws for the common internal market, which no other international organization can. This is important, because nation states have always resisted losing their competitive advantage over other nation states. Even in the field of taxation, which has been kept as a national prerogative in the EU, for the aforementioned reason, tax harmonization has taken place within the EU, for example on a converging value-added tax rate. The EU is also a good example, because it was founded from the outset on liberal market values, much more than on competing socialist values. One reason for this was precisely the history of oppression all the founding members of the EU had suffered under the Nazis during the Second World War. Freedom in political terms, embodied in democracy, became the unshakeable foundation of the EU, an ideal Hayek defended passionately in *The Road to Serfdom*. Whether the corresponding liberal market ideas are equally convincing will be considered in this book.

1

From the Eighteenth to the Twentieth Century: Momentous Change and Stable Elements

H ayek's spiritual fathers are clearly those working in the classical liberal tradition arguing for the economic freedoms of the middle classes. Hayek often quotes Lord Acton and other notable liberal politicians and thinkers, highly reputable at the time, but in the end such applied liberalism takes him and us back inexorably to the great ideas of liberalism elaborated, promoted or developed by John Stuart Mill, Adam Smith, David Hume and even the conservative Edmund Burke.[1] These thinkers expressed their ideas of economic freedom differently, such as purely in terms of supply and demand, in terms of the market as the final arbiter, or taking the view that 'the unrestrained freedom of buying and selling is the great animating principle of production and supply.'[2] Essentially, however, they all endorsed an untrammelled free market as the ideal venue for economic activity resulting in a free society.

In conjunction with classical liberal theory, Hayek saw the main paradox of the economy and human society in the fact that they seem to work well even though no one is in control of them:

> economics has come nearer than any other social science to an answer to that central question of all social sciences, how the combination of fragments of knowledge existing in different minds can bring about results which, if they were to be brought about deliberately, would require a

knowledge on the part of the directing mind which no single person can possess.[3]

Such a statement brings us very close to Smith's invisible hand, of course.[4] The fascinating logic of liberalism is, in fact, that of 'irreducible subjective perceptions'.[5] Classical liberals accepted that and saw the plethora of knowledge and resulting opinions as an asset of their theory, in which the individual takes his decisions on the basis of his subjective judgement as to how to maximize profit for himself. Edmund Burke described the market logic, which connects all these individual positions, in the following way:

> The balance between consumption and production makes price. The market settles, and alone can settle, that price. Market is the meeting and conference of the *consumer* and *producer*, when they mutually discover each other's wants. Nobody, I believe, has observed with any reflection what market is, without being astonished at the truth, the correctness, the celerity, the general equity, with which the balance of wants is settled.[6]

This means that at the origin of all economic activity there is a knowledge problem of the individual actor in the market – what would now be called a problem of 'market transparency'.[7] Under a liberal logic, individual expectations are connected and can work to the advantage of society only through the market: 'Hayek argued that market pricing provided the only adequate indicator of relative scarcity: having abolished market pricing, planners could not adequately assess opportunity costs and calculate relative scarcities.'[8] Hayek believes in a market logic which, in a way very similar to Smith's invisible hand, transcends individual human comprehension and can never be grasped by human understanding, because it is too complex. Nevertheless, it works, however imperfectly, reasonably well in the market. The market as the connection between all individual human reasoning is thus necessary for human progress. Keynes, in his *General Theory*, agrees with the idea of the coordinating function of the market, but also observes inbuilt imperfections:

> it is an outstanding characteristic of the economic system in which we live that, whilst it is subject to severe fluctuations in respect of output and employment, it is not violently unstable. Indeed it seems capable of remaining in a chronic condition of sub-normal activity for a considerable period without any marked tendency either towards recovery or towards complete collapse. Moreover, the evidence indicates that full, or even approximately full, employment is of rare and short-lived occurrence. Fluctuations may start briskly but seem to wear themselves out before they have proceeded to great extremes, and an intermediate situation which is neither desperate nor satisfactory is our normal lot.[9]

The First World War had already changed this evaluation, at least for Keynes. However, at the time of writing *The Road to Serfdom*, Hayek would defend the merits of classical liberalism, which he called 'the abandoned road'[10] – 'abandoned' because these liberal teachings were often considered to be part of the reason for the Great Depression which had led to the Second World War. Keynesianism became the way out of the crisis, and it is not surprising that we find Keynes sharing this criticism of classical liberal teachings: 'The difficulty lies not in the new ideas, but in escaping from the old ones, which ramify, for those brought up as most of us have been, into every corner of our minds.'[11] Hayek, in contrast, mourned the demise of classical liberal values, the merits of which he defended in his description of the two strands of classical liberalism, as described in the following.

On the one hand, economic liberalism argues that the market will provide the maximum incentive for entrepreneurship, private initiative and personal profit. This leads to the conclusion that the market must also provide the best possible outcome for society and its citizens, because it stimulates active forces within society so that they produce wealth. In its turn, this will be to the common benefit, through a 'trickle-down' effect of accumulated wealth seeping through from the top to the bottom of society. Edmund Burke gave the following example:

> But if the farmer [representing the entrepreneur] is excessively avaricious? – why, so much the better – the more he desires to increase his gains, the more interested is he in the good condition of those, upon whose labour his gains must principally depend.[12]

This also means that eventually generated wealth can be taxed by government authorities and can be redistributed. However, the idea of taxation is already a qualification of the original concept of liberalism, which holds that the market should be allowed to operate entirely untrammelled in order to satisfy the economic needs of society – call it laissez-faire, Manchester capitalism or simply the free market economy.[13] For liberals, the function of the market is to satisfy society's needs, which has nothing to do with poverty – which was, rather, the normal state of affairs, the way mankind had always lived. At the height of the Industrial Revolution in the early nineteenth century, poverty was rampant and part of daily life. It led classical liberals such as Edmund Burke to state that the masses were poor because there was not enough produce for everyone to be well fed. The rich were few. Taking away their fortune would change nothing about the plight of the poor, because in comparison, the masses were too big and their fortunes too small. This is the basis of the concept of scarcity, which had been inherent in any human society the classical liberals knew of. This logic also poised the rich as facilitators, people who could lend money for investment and who thus made the economy work.[14] The pertinence of this argument was based on the experience of real life. Even Keynes toed the same line in his earlier works, such as *The Economic Consequences of the*

Peace (1919).[15] Burke effectively says that there have always been the rich and there have always been the poor in society and that this is not likely to change, because the poor masses, just like the rich few, have important functions in society. This rationale may still be true for relative poverty today, in which, with the advent of the welfare state, no one in Western industrialized societies actually goes hungry, but where participation in society for the relatively poor remains difficult, because of the uneven distribution of opportunities and parental wealth.

On the other hand, liberalism also means 'civil liberty'. This second strand of liberalism advocates fundamental freedoms. This has to be seen against the background of the eighteenth- and nineteenth-century emancipation of the emerging middle classes from aristocratic privilege and arbitrary or tyrannical royal power. Liberalism, at its root, is liberation from the shackles and bonds imposed by surviving feudal regimes. The middle class, the bourgeoisie and the intelligentsia saw their inner drive for advancement hindered by the old order of social status, rank and an aristocratic constitutional order. The seeds of the Enlightenment promised progress, the spread of knowledge, the spirit of toleration, the rule of law, liberty and even democracy. In the eighteenth century, the winds of change brought the old order under heavy strain and laid bare its weaknesses. Towards the end of the century, some monarchies were clearly threatened. The French Revolution was, among many other things, a lucid demonstration that the *ancien régime* was not only 'the *former* system' but a system that had become thoroughly discredited and hopelessly out of date.

Even before that, the intellectual inventiveness of the burgeoning middle classes had developed in academia, because new ideas concerning the organization of the 'good' society found fertile ground in universities. Such natural receptiveness in places such as Oxford and Cambridge could, however, only be gradual, because colleges and universities were originally set up to serve the aristocratic system by preparing the scions of wealthy families to take over positions of power. Hence, conservatism – in the sense of conservation of the existing system – was slow to admit new ideas as to how the economy and the state should be run. Moreover, such conservatism permeated almost all aspects of society. The only point at which the constraints of vested class interests could readily be broken was in the realm of the economy, because profit did not ask for station in society. No status, title, office or social rank could provide real profit, and certainly not the productive generation of wealth. Private initiative, ideas and entrepreneurship could do that. And with earned profit, the middle classes could slowly but surely *buy* their civil liberty. Here we find the radical element in liberalism, which we still find in raptor capitalism – that is, profit at any cost – today. The energy within it comes from the will to gain *more*; in the original case to gain more freedom. The right to pursue one's own happiness comes from this desire for freedom, as expressed in the United States Constitution, which postulated the free pursuit of happiness; although for a time, Edmund Burke, among others, thought that the persistent drive to possess more was essentially a sign of vulgarity:

> Whether what may be called moral or philosophical happiness of the laborious classes is increased or not, I cannot say. The seat of that species of happiness is in the mind; and there are few data to ascertain the comparative state of mind at any two periods. Philosophical happiness is to want little. Civil or vulgar happiness is to want much, and enjoy much.[16]

This misapprehension of the power of profit to enable one to achieve more freedom was reflected in the low esteem accorded to trading, and therefore the trader. However, the desire for more, as I called it above, must be seen as the original driving force behind liberalism as an ideology, which tried to change the rigid societal structures into which it was born.

Hayek goes back to this root and defines it as the only reasonable foundation for the 'good' life in the 'good society' – while conceding some qualifications for the benefit of the disadvantaged (considered later in this book). He reasoned that state intervention in the economy can only pervert the genuinely positive drive of individuals to achieve profit. By serving themselves by making more profit, they serve everyone else too. State intervention, on the contrary, cannot be stopped once started, because one needs more and more antidote to remedy the original wrong of state intervention or even economic planning, Hayek argued. To prevent citizens from following their own interests – quite simply, profit – was thus the wrong approach. More and more state intervention necessarily means less and less freedom, leading inevitably, in the first instance, to the 'nanny state'. Eventually the process must lead to dictatorship, if equal access to resources and opportunities is to be achieved. All freedom is lost, including the personal freedoms postulated by liberalism. What Hayek is thus describing is the trade-off between the goal of equality – be it of opportunity or of outcome – among citizens and the goal of individual freedom. This is a trade-off which *every* society in history has had to make, Hayek argued, and for his part, he leans heavily on the side of freedom.

Keynes would mostly agree with the commitment to freedom, but, for the sake of stability, he would advocate an economic framework set by the state within which economic freedom can be enjoyed. Stability, foreseeability and predictability of the economy, rather than the absolute income of the worker, are really the key elements in both theories. In modern societies, money is the tool to achieve this. This led Keynes to the recommendation 'That money-wages [the nominal figure of wage] should be more stable than real wages [what one can buy with one's money] is a condition of the system possessing inherent stability.'[17] We see this implemented today in the general preference for indirect taxation, notably, value-added tax, rather than direct taxation of remunerations, where nominal wages – what Keynes called 'money-wage' – increase, but real wages not necessarily so, because of inflation or indirect taxation. However, it also reflects the experience that reducing real wages has its limits. It will meet very understandable popular resistance when the wage, regardless of whether money-wage or real wage, is no longer enough to live on; a noteworthy example is that of the current crisis in Greece. In monetary regimes before the Eurozone, which has strict management of inflation, it would also have been preferable to concede a degree of inflation rather than see money-wages reduced. The reason given by Keynes for this is that such a policy does not upset the expectation of stability:

> the expectation of a relative stickiness of wages in terms of money is a corollary of the excess of liquidity-premium over carrying costs being greater for money than for any other asset . . . The fact that money has low elasticities of production and substitution and low carrying-costs tends to raise the expectation that [it] will be relatively stable; and this expectation enhances money's liquidity-premium . . . [18]

With reference to classical liberalism, Keynes also shows that money has not always been the only means of payment. In feudal societies, compensation for services provided was often made in the form of land, for reasons similar to those why money is used in modern societies, that is, very low elasticity of production and substitution. Therefore, high rates of interest could be charged for its use, as they can be for money.[19] Against the backdrop of classical economic theory, it is important to understand at this point that money is merely a means to the end of facilitating economic exchange in society. In a liberal context, profit would be the ultimate goal of economic activity, but where economic theory becomes a description of human society the following caveat should be added: 'Not all of organized human activity need be motivated by profit . . . [for example,] voluntary associations.'[20] Naturally, this qualification comes from critics of (neo-)liberalism, in which profit seems to be the main motive for economic action; but can it be the only one? We have to look for the answer to the question of whether economic theory should become a *social* theory once again, as it was in the classical economic analyses of Smith, Mill and Marx. There are examples in the real economy of situations where profit is not the only objective, notably in charities or social businesses, and generally in non-profit organizations, however suspect some of them may seem from a liberal market perspective.

In the following, we will see what Hayek added to classical liberal theory in an economic sense, but we will also consider the malfunctioning of societies, a target of Hayek's vigorous criticism. This criticism is clear evidence of his social aspirations and, generally, a desire for a better world; by 1944, towards the end of the Second World War, when he was writing *The Road to Serfdom*, this was a self-evident motive.

2

Hayek's Road to Liberty

The price function is the key to and the fulcrum of Hayek's liberal economy. He spells this out very clearly as the core of the working economy. No economic actor can know all the details, that could logically influence his rational choice in the market, simply because the whole economy is too complex to be comprehensible to anyone. Because of that, the economy escapes what Hayek calls 'conscious control'.[1] The price of a product, the price which someone is willing to take and someone else is willing to spend, is the coordination of the expectations of the former and the latter actor. No system has been found that could fulfil that important function of coordinating supply and demand but the market.[2] Untrammelled competition in the marketplace is essential if this balancing act between buyer and seller is to yield the 'right' price. The objective becomes that of profit maximization by means of keen, competitive pricing, that is, low prices more than offset by high turnover to yield enough profit to keep the economic agent in the market. This logic triggers individual action in the economy in order to materialize profit. Hayek is clearly in line with classical liberal theory here:

> But who are to judge what that profit and advantage ought to be? Certainly no authority on earth. It is a matter of convention dictated by the reciprocal convenience of the parties, and indeed by their reciprocal necessities.[3]

This anonymous process of price determination is, for Hayek, the foundation on which the modern economy rests and thus on which society is built. To fulfil the needs of modern society, extensive division of labour became necessary and thus the complexity of modern societies has been possible only on the basis of a system of a liberal market economy which is not planned but rather fulfils the anonymous function of setting the right price at the right time for the right product.[4]

> That the division of labour has reached the extent which makes modern civilisation possible we owe to the fact that it did not have to be consciously created, but that man stumbled on a method by which the division of labour could be extended far beyond the limits within which it could have been planned. Any further growth of its complexity, therefore, far from making central direction more necessary, makes it more important than ever that we should use a technique which does not depend on conscious control.[5]

In this passage Hayek draws the conclusion that modern society – seen as inherently positive – can only continue its path of growth on the basis of economic freedom and individual liberty (one might well invoke the image of Adam Smith's invisible hand here[6]). Importantly, what is meant is freedom and liberty in the economic sense as well as the political sense. The link between the economic and the political sides of liberalism is Hayek's equation: more economic planning = less freedom; more freedom = more progress of the positive type liberalism had provided. This was the liberalism that had transformed societies of the type of the *ancien régime* into *modern* societies. It leads Hayek's liberal economic theory and even some critics of neoliberal doctrine to the conclusion that 'Wholesale planning is incapable of adequately coordinating "the actions of scattered individuals, each of whom is in possession of unique, partial, tacit and potentially erroneous knowledge."'[7] And this ties in nicely with Ricardo's idea of comparative advantage – in this case, of the individual who has certain knowledge over another individual who does not have that knowledge.[8]

The focus on the individual actor in liberalism led to the development of individualism. The individual's perspective on the world is seen as specific, and therefore potentially economically advantageous, and thus eventually exploitable for his or her own economic profit: 'individuals have a partially tacit and unique understanding of the world surrounding them, and production does not take place according to engineering manuals. There is thus no way to centralize all useful knowledge.'[9] The lack of comprehensive knowledge of the market makes central planning of the economy impossible, and the individual economic actor is the only one capable of making sense of the specifically relevant information for their particular economic situation:

> I shall label this theme by saying that there is an 'epistemic gap' between the way the world is and our apprehension of it, and often even more so, between the way that the world will unfold in the future and our anticipations of its unfolding … we are not passive receptors of signals from the outside world, but interpret and infer things from information we receive in an active and, above all, highly selective way.[10]

This uncertainty, which only the individual can manage for a specific situation, is perhaps the strongest argument of liberalism in favour of the market and against central planning. 'Most significantly, it is an insight that would have to make one sceptical of the feasibility and benefits of national economic planning. And that is before we consider twentieth century economic history.'[11]

There are, however, also limitations to this liberal logic. Hayek concedes a possible exemption from the near-absolute dominion of the price-competition mechanism: in the introduction of new technologies which are genuinely beneficial but not yet economically viable. Here is a situation where government start-up protection and subsidies are, he argues, justified, because such technologies will bring improvements. They can reasonably be expected to become economically profitable in the near future.[12] However, such circumstances, in Hayek's view, rather reinforce the paradigm of competition in its superiority to planning, because they are really only exceptions to the normal beneficial running of the economy.[13]

Struggling to achieve acceptance of his re-interpretation of classical liberalism by fellow academics and others in positions of responsibility and power, Hayek saw one of the major reasons for the widespread demand for economic planning in the 1930s and '40s in the imperfection of human nature, or, more specifically, in a vain and ultimately counter-productive striving for perfection.

> There is an infinite number of good things, which we all agree are highly desirable as well as possible, but of which we cannot hope to achieve more than a few within our lifetime, or which we can hope to achieve only very imperfectly. It is the frustration of his ambition in his own field which makes the specialist revolt against the existing order. We all find it difficult to bear to see things left undone which everybody must admit are both desirable and possible.[14]

Here, Hayek sees utopia as a futile objective of human action, just as he denounced socialism as an inherently elusive idealism which leads to evils greater than it could ever have hoped to remedy in the first place.[15] This is a very cold message, as many politicians after the Second World War realized. If the market were only numbers and profit, the weaker elements of society would always rebel against it, because of the inherent prejudice in the free market economy in favour of the stronger players.[16] In the post-war period, this led to an almost universal consensus approving the creation of the welfare state, most notably in the National Health Service in Britain.[17] This was based on the realization that the modern market economy needed a social element. Even staunchly conservative politicians such as Charles de Gaulle in France accepted that the modern economy needs a face which, as he put it, is not made of steel.[18] Otherwise, the whole system will fail to generate, much less deserve, loyalty or commitment, a consideration which became particularly important in the ideological competition with communism during the Cold War.

That did not mean, however, that one should engage in ideas of creating a modern utopia. The idealistic view of the merits of economic planning was open to corruption, Hayek argued, pointing to the German *Autobahnen*, which were widely applauded as a tremendous technical and social achievement at the time; in reality, Hitler had had them built in the first instance for military purposes.[19] Such dictatorial corruption for evil ideals was the sickness of the time in which Hayek and Keynes wrote their main works. Hayek shows very clearly the threat that the unmoderated drive for a single objective, such as in a totalitarian state or a modern utopia, posed:

> The movement for planning owes its present strength largely to the fact that, while planning is in the main still an ambition, it unites almost all the single-minded idealists, all the men and women who have devoted their lives to a single task. The hopes they are placing in planning, however, are not the result of a comprehensive view of society, but rather a very limited view . . . But it would make the very men who are most anxious to plan society the most dangerous if they were allowed to do so – and the most intolerant of the planning of others . . . there could hardly be a more unbearable – more irrational – world than one in which the most eminent specialists in each field were allowed to proceed unchecked with the realisation of their ideals.[20]

Beyond the suspicion of experts and idealists, this argument sees compromise – as in the British parliamentary model – as the only sensible political system. It dovetails very neatly into the idea of the

Member of Parliament as an amateur who has to care for the whole of society. The MP can never be as good as the experts in their fields, but they are responsible for making the links with sources of expert knowledge, for the good of all society. Liberals of all persuasions would agree with Hayek that society is a common living space for all, which must not be dominated by one man, or one interest. At the time, this was diametrically opposed to Hitler's credo of one, *Ein Volk, ein Reich, ein Führer*, because this is, in Hayek's view, the dangerous final consequence of expert planning, which leads inescapably to totalitarianism.

From this realization Hayek drew the unflinching commitment to freedom. In economic terms, Hayek's converse argument would be that democracy needs the free market to guarantee freedom in society:

> the institution of private property is one of the main things that have given man that limited amount of free-and-equalness that Marx hoped to render infinite by abolishing this institution. Strangely enough Marx was the first to see this. He is the one who informed us, looking backwards, that the evolution of private capitalism with its free market had been a precondition for the evolution of all our democratic freedoms. It never occurred to him, looking forward, that if this was so, these other freedoms might disappear with the abolition of the free market.[21]

Hayek thus modified classical liberalism in certain aspects while accepting the basic premise that value must first be produced in order to be shared out. Only then can the yield in added value the employees create be distributed, at least in part, to them. And only then will they make the rational choice to work, to create and therefore to earn part of the added value. In the Austrian school of economics, of which Hayek became the most important representative in the twentieth century, this eventually feeds into a theory of rational choice by economic actors as well as by the individual worker:[22]

But there are a number of different aspects of human agency that crop up repeatedly in Austrian writings. Prominent amongst these is the purposeful and goal-directed nature of human action, the capacity to form mental images of possible future events, the capacity for choice between alternative courses of action, alertness, surprise, judgement, boldness and error.[23]

These are considered in liberal economic theory as the specific capabilities of the individual, which make their action in the economy unique and authentic. In liberalism, this becomes a belief that such human skills cannot be captured in mathematical abstraction or a universal plan – the

assumption that actors' beliefs are legitimately represented by classical probability functions. Proponents of Austrian Economics criticise this assumption on two fronts. In the first place, they argue that stable relative frequencies are rarely to be found in the social realm, that most ordinary individuals would have difficulty in estimating them even if they were, and that they are in any event of limited usefulness in one-shot decision situations. It then follows that situations in which actors' choices are actually guided by a knowledge of objective probabilities are likely to be the exception rather than the rule.[24]

Individual decisions about making a certain product, for example, therefore are seldom based on the complete information necessary to make that decision, but the decision to make the product is nevertheless taken. The connecting element linking all these imperfect decisions is the market, and in it the price for a specific product. Success or failure in the free market then becomes the final judgement as to whether an entrepreneurial decision was good or bad in an economic sense, that is, profit-making or loss-making.

This was the classical liberal argument from the supply side. Keynes turned Hayek's rationale on its head, starting not from the point of view of value creation, but from that of the benefit for society and, specifically, for those in, or aspiring to, gainful employment. Keynes admits that 'there will always exist in a non-static society a proportion of [human] resources [left idle] "between jobs".'[25] He describes this as 'involuntary' unemployment;[26] a figure which would usually be set at around 4 per cent in industrialized societies today. However, Keynes next turns to the 'means of increasing employment',[27] while the classical school and Hayek would consider the conditions necessary for creating goods, leading to economic growth in the first place. The classical liberal argument would state that the wage of a worker depends on the price paid for the product itself, determined by supply and demand on the market and thus the worker's productivity.[28] Keynes cast this fundamental contention into doubt:

> the contention that the unemployment which characterizes a depression is due to a refusal by labor to accept a reduction of money-wages is not clearly supported by the facts. It is not very plausible to assert that unemployment in the United States in 1932 was due either to labor obstinately refusing to accept a reduction of money-wage or to its obstinately demanding a real wage beyond what the productivity of the economic machine was capable of furnishing. Wide variations are experienced in the volume of employment without any apparent change either in the minimum real demands of labor or in its productivity. Labor is not more truculent in the depression than in the boom – far from it. Nor is its physical productivity less. These facts from experience are a *prima facie* ground for questioning the adequacy of the classical analysis.[29]

Rather than cutting wages, as happened in the Great Depression, Keynes argues that the state should intervene in the economy by using monetary policy – moderating the quantity of money[30] – or by adapting interest rates. The employers based in classical liberal theory carried on demanding flexibility of wages from workers and corresponding state regulation.[31] They had done this during the Depression and it prevented neither the virtual breakdown of industry, nor the resulting mass unemployment and its corresponding social misery. With that analysis Keynes contested a core tenet of free market economics: that the market will eventually self-regulate and that unfettered market activity will consistently lead to the best outcome for all. Keynes turns this argument on its head and makes of it his moral case for state intervention.[32] Keynes argues, disagreeing with Hayek, that the free market economy can function only in authoritarian regimes and that state intervention in the economy will consequently ensure that democracies do not drift towards authoritarian rule:

> To suppose that a flexible wage policy is a right and proper adjunct of a system which on the whole is one of *laissez-faire*, is the opposite of the truth. It is only in a highly authoritarian society, where sudden, substantial, all-round changes could be decreed, that a flexible wage-policy could function with success. One can imagine it in operation in Italy, Germany or Russia, but not in France, the United States or Great Britain.[33]

It is clear that both Hayek and Keynes found the political development of authoritarian regimes and dictatorship, as happened in the 1930s and '40s, wholly abhorrent. Both saw at least part of the reason for this phenomenon in maladministration of the economy. However, the remedies they proposed were diametrically opposed. On the one hand, Keynes proposed state intervention in the economy through monetary policy and variation of interest rates, for example, so that the economy would find the right economic environment to generate and foster a degree of output corresponding to full employment. On the other, Hayek saw the economic freedom of liberalism as the precondition for retaining the political freedoms enjoyed by people in Britain and other Western democracies at the time. What was happening in authoritarian and totalitarian regimes, as for example in his home country, Austria – which had in effect been annexed by the Third Reich in 1938 – was exactly the opposite.

Unfortunately for Hayek, by the time he was writing *The Road to Serfdom*, Britain and the United States, too, were running their economies on a war footing, that is, as highly planned economies. These circumstances would not foster the popularity of the free market philosophy Hayek was proposing; rather the opposite. Thus he found himself a lonely Cassandra, fated to be ignored, warning of the evils that could come from economic planning. He was unable to stem the tide of more planning, imposed on Western governments through their war effort. Even more frustrating for Hayek, planning plainly produced the desired results, for example in the U.S. Victory Program, which geared the U.S. economy towards winning the Second World War. Even before the United States entered the war, Franklin D. Roosevelt proposed the New Deal for American workers and the American economy, which had repercussions long into the post-war period. Keynesianism became the dominant economic doctrine and Hayek's ideas of a free market economy were largely sidelined until the 1970s. Only with the 1973 oil crisis, marking the end of the golden post-war years of growing prosperity, and the poor performance of Western economies still run along Keynesian principles, did liberal market ideas become popular again. Hayek's ideas were turned into what we know today as neoliberalism. By the mid-1970s, Keynesianism was widely considered bankrupt, and governments, particularly in Britain and the United States, were looking for other models. Hayek, who long outlived Keynes, was there at the birth of the new orthodoxy.

3
Information and Planning

B right and entrepreneurial as he was, Hayek took the opportunity to develop his liberal ideas against the backdrop of the more promising political environment of the 1970s. One of the most lucid insights in Hayek's liberalism is the question: why are we ever right? Or, how do a thousand pieces make a whole? These fundamental questions take him back to the original question of the social sciences and therefore also of economics: how does society work? Classical liberalism had given some answers, but similar questions were also posed in politics, namely in Jean-Jacques Rousseau's *The Social Contract*, where the will of all (*volonté de tous*) is distinguished from the general will (*volonté générale*). It is really only this general will that makes a people and brings them together for a common good.[1] Hayek was puzzled, as Adam Smith had been so long before: how can the separate and independent actions of individuals add up to what amounts to a detailed and deliberate plan for their economic actions and, more importantly, how can this unexplained phenomenon accommodate and indeed foster the creation of a stable economy, and with it a stable society in which human beings can thrive? Hayek considered this problem early in his seminal essay 'Economics and Knowledge', which was first given as a presidential address to the London Economic Club on 10 November 1936, and was then published in *Economica* in February 1937.[2] He put it as follows:

The problem which we pretend [to] solve is how the spontaneous interaction of a number of people, each possessing
only bits of knowledge, brings about a state of affairs in
which prices correspond to costs, etc., and which could be
brought about by deliberate direction only by somebody
who possessed the combined knowledge of all those individuals. And experience shows us that something of this
sort does happen, since the empirical observation that
prices do tend to correspond to costs was the beginning of
the science. But in our analysis, instead of showing what
bits of information the different persons must possess in
order to bring about that result, we fall in effect back on
the assumption that everybody knows everything and so
evade any real solution of the problem.[3]

From the analysis of a knowledge gap, Hayek started his inquiry
into the information necessary to make economic decisions. This led
him to the question of how foresight works, by criticizing traditional
equilibrium analysis, the theory of risk and the theory of imperfect
competition.[4] We do not need to go into any of these theories in
detail, because their main elements will be explained in Hayek's own
arguments. What is important at the outset, however, is that this
criticism leads him to turn the classical question of economics on
its head; that is, the question of why, and how, people can make the
right predictions and take consequent action.[5] 'The situation seems
here to be that before we can explain why people make mistakes, we
must first explain why they should ever be right.'[6] He argues that the
concept of equilibrium is essentially based on expectations of the
stability of the economy, which all economic actors share and use
as the basis for their decisions in the economy.[7] Hayek argues that
these expectations of stability are modelled on the current reality in
which the actors live and which they are trying to preserve, because
that is what they know. They want to preserve it, because they think
that they can manage their current reality. This leads to a desire for

equilibrium rather than change. One could call this a self-fulfilling prophecy – or what Hayek calls 'tautologies' – created by the human desire for stability.[8] Economic actors then develop their own plans as to how to turn economic equilibrium to their personal advantage.[9] Upsetting the equilibrium is not in the interests of the economic actors, because they have made the rational choice to use it for their own profit: 'any change in the relevant knowledge of the person, that is, any change which leads him to alter his plan, disrupts the equilibrium relation between his actions taken before and those taken after the change in his knowledge.'[10] Thus under normal circumstances, economic actors try to preserve stability over time and adjust their actions so that the economy remains in equilibrium.[11]

However, equilibrium analysis was originally introduced to describe the idea of balance between the actions of different people.[12] In other words, 'equilibrium in this connection exists if the actions of all members of society over a period are all executions of their respective individual plans on which each decided at the beginning of the period.'[13] But, according to this definition, equilibrium can hardly ever exist, unless there is an overarching entity to which all expectations, and the corresponding plans of individuals, are attuned:[14]

> In the first instance, in order that all these plans can be carried out, it is necessary for them to be based on the expectations of the same set of external events, since, if different people were to base their plans on conflicting expectations, no set of external events could make the execution of all these plans possible. And, second, in a society based on exchange their plans will to a considerable extent refer to actions which require corresponding actions on the part of other individuals. This means that the plans of different individuals must in a special sense be compatible.[15]

Against the background of the previous chapters, the reader would expect this overarching entity to be the free market, but

Hayek's explanation is rather more complex, involving the concepts of objective and subjective data:

> There seems to be no possible doubt that these two concepts of 'data', on the one hand in the sense of objective real facts, as the observing economist is supposed to know them, and on the other in the subjective sense, as things known to the persons whose behaviour we try to explain, are really fundamentally different and ought to be kept carefully apart. And, as we shall see, the question why the data in the subjective sense of the term should ever come to correspond to the objective data is one of the main problems we have to answer.[16]

This definition raises the question of whether there can ever be an objective set of data. Hans-Georg Gadamer, relying on his theory of hermeneutics, would at this point question the very existence of 'truth', and would instead stress the relativity of truth to the individual perspective.[17] This means that only the combination of subjectivities enables us to approach objectivity. Consequently, empirical analysis of expectations is vital and only the combination of alternative versions of (economic) reality will produce objectivity, which then becomes, to a considerable extent, the reality we live in. Thus equilibrium does not mean the absence of change. It only means that expectations stay stable. Hayek offers a pertinent example in the change of seasons, which everyone 'expects'.[18] In an economic context, this means that there are certain expectations of economic development which produce equilibrium in society.[19] Every society must therefore be based on the experience of the same reality by its citizens.

> There would of course be no reason why the subjective data of different people should ever correspond unless they were due to the experience of the same objective facts . . . The equilibrium relationship cannot be deduced merely from

the objective facts, since the analysis of what people will do can only start from what is known to them. Nor can equilibrium analysis start merely from a given set of subjective data, since the subjective data of different people would be either compatible or incompatible, that is, they would already determine whether equilibrium did or did not exist.[20]

Here Hayek reaches the limits of economics as a social science, mimicking the natural sciences when he says that our subjective data – which could also be called individual reality – can only either correspond or not. However, the objection must be made at this point that human realities or expectations are not either right or wrong. They cannot be captured by binary mathematics, but must use social science methods, according to which an empirical analysis may be made in order to determine which parts of our subjective data do or do not correspond to other sets.

Hayek's problem at this point of his analysis is that a binary mathematical answer cannot give an answer to a much more complex social reality – indeed, this is also the current problem of economics itself, in modelling and formalizing the discipline. Social sciences, in their different forms, would argue for a search of a social consensus or core values of a society, on which individuals would orient their expectations.[21] Hayek goes some way in this direction and remedies his problem through an

admittedly fictitious state of equilibrium . . . the only justification for this is the supposed existence of a tendency towards equilibrium. It is only with this assertion that economics ceases to be an exercise in pure logic and becomes an empirical science.[22]

Importantly, this is an empirical science in the sense of *social* sciences, because social phenomena of human society are then essentially the subject of empirical investigations in economics.

This led Hayek to the question of defining equilibrium, both in the economic and the social sense, which eventually also leads to factors which foster political equilibrium. Human action is based on experience of what works and what does not in real life: 'it is only relative to the knowledge which a person is bound to acquire in the course of the carrying out of his original plan and its successive alterations that an equilibrium is likely to be reached.'[23] This happens against the background of generally applicable expectations, which could be called core consensus or values, and which would usually be enshrined in constitutional documents. From there,

> the expectations of the people and particularly of the entrepreneurs will become more and more correct. In this form the assertion of the existence of a tendency towards equilibrium is clearly an empirical proposition, that is, an assertion about what happens in the real world which ought, at least in principle, to be capable of verification.[24]

From this, one can assume rational choice as the basis of human action, based on facts according to which humans act.[25] This leads Hayek back to the need for economic actors to know facts, or to the problem of knowledge: 'how much knowledge and what sort of knowledge the different individuals must possess in order that we may be able to speak of equilibrium. It is clear that if the concept is to have any empirical significance it cannot presuppose that everybody knows everything.'[26] This really captures the key problem of any economic actor – namely, incomplete information, or subjective truth. Hayek's pertinent question is, then: who has to know what, and when and how? This he calls the 'division of knowledge' in society:

> Clearly there is here a problem of the *division of knowledge* which is quite analogous to, and at least as important as, the problem of the division of labour. But while the latter has been one of the main subjects of investigation ever since the

beginning of our science, the former has been as completely neglected, although it seems to me to be the really central problem of economics as a social science.[27]

The knowledge necessary for economic decisions is not confined merely to prices, but really comprises a much larger general knowledge of society and thus the economy; for example, 'the knowledge of the basic fact of how different commodities can be obtained and used'.[28] Hayek summarized the problem of knowledge as the link between subjective data and objective facts. This link is assumed to exist naturally, but must be defined empirically for each separate economic actor if one wants to arrive at a comprehensive understanding of the economy.[29] Eventually, we find ourselves back at the question of how all of human (economic) action works together. For Hayek, it is the market and its unique capacity to determine the 'right' price; for political scientists, such as Isaiah Berlin, it may be consensus and core values; for philosophers such as Jürgen Habermas and Hans-Georg Gadamer, it may be discourse, or the interpretation of reality by individuals, respectively.[30] We will see in the next chapter that Keynes sees this overarching entity, which unites everything and makes economic actors work together, as the fiscal, monetary and general economic framework the state provides so that individual economic actors can work productively within it.

4
Keynes's General Theory

Keynes put this logic together in *The General Theory of Employment, Interest and Money*. This book is probably his most important work and is, therefore, the principal focus in this chapter.

This theory can be summed up in the following propositions:

(1) In a given situation of technique, resources and costs, income (both money-income and real income) depends on the volume of employment N.

(2) . . . consumption will depend on the level of aggregate income and, therefore, on the level of employment N, except when there is some change in the propensity to consume.

. . .

(5) Hence, the volume of employment in equilibrium depends on (i) the aggregate supply function, f (ii) the propensity to consume, c, and (iii) the volume of investment, D_2. This is the essence of the General Theory of Employment.

. . .

(8) . . . the economic system may well find itself in stable equilibrium with N at a level below full employment, namely at the level given by the intersection of the aggregate demand function with the aggregate supply function.[1]

Keynes effectively says that if supply and the propensity to consume remain relatively stable, the key to full employment is the volume of investment. This can be directed by the state. Against the background of the Great Depression, Keynes argues that the state has a moral obligation to invest in order to serve the people. The mass unemployment experienced during the Great Depression has to be avoided in the future, because of its dire consequences – of which the Second World War was seen as the most serious. Keynes put it in the language of the economist as follows:

> The propensity to consume and the rate of new investment determine between them the volume of employment, and the volume of employment is uniquely related to a given level of real wages – not the other way round ... This analysis supplies us with an explanation of the paradox of poverty in the midst of plenty. For the mere existence of an insufficiency of effective demand may, and often will, bring the increase of employment to a standstill *before* a level of full employment has been reached ... Moreover the richer the community, the wider will tend to be the gap between its actual and its potential production; and therefore the more obvious and outrageous the defects of the economic system.[2]

'Poverty in the midst of plenty' summarized famously the plight of Western societies in the 1930s. Keynes was determined to establish the economic reasons for this phenomenon and elaborate viable solutions to it.

This led Keynes to the most controversial policy during the Depression, namely 'deficit spending'. Many states were deeply indebted and could no longer find lenders on the free market. The Weimar Republic was a dramatic example. However, keeping the subsequent political radicalization of Germany in mind, Keynes advocated deficit spending as the lesser of two evils. 'For a man who has been long unemployed some measure of labor, instead of involving disutility, may have a positive utility. If this is accepted, the above reasoning shows how "wasteful" loan expenditure may nevertheless enrich the community on balance.'[3] Keynes's economic idea here is that the state should rather subsidize employment than pay for unemployment, nor should it leave its citizens in abject poverty, because in that situation they cannot fulfil any positive function for society. By financing employment the state would foster economic growth and therefore overall social well-being. Beyond economics, what is really at stake here is the stability of society, and this means avoiding a political drift towards authoritarian rule or dictatorships, as happened in 1933 in Germany. Economically, Keynes argued that if the state is able to stimulate consumption, it should do so: 'For we have seen that, up to the point where full employment prevails, the growth of capital depends not at all on the low propensity to consume but is, on the contrary, held back by it.'[4] The concept of deficit spending went completely against anything that classical economic theory, wedded to the ideals of laissez-faire and non-interference in the markets, could entertain. And there was proof that his concept worked, because Keynes's argument also summarizes what was implemented in the New Deal policy in the United States in the 1930s and '40s.[5]

One key element of the economic framework Keynes demanded was to set the interest rate relatively low, in order to stimulate investment. State control of interest rates thus played an important role in Keynesian economics. The basic definition of it is very simple:

> the mere definition of the rate of interest tells us in so many words that the rate of interest is, in itself, nothing more than the inverse proportion between a sum of money and what can be obtained for parting with control over the money in exchange for debt for a stated period of time.[6]

From the point of view of an individual creditor or debtor, this is straightforward, but it does not explain the role of interest rates in the economic policy of a state. Classical economists had written whole treatises on the subject, analyses with which Keynes was, unsurprisingly, not content about the dominant

> theory of the rate of interest. The justification for a moderately high rate of interest has been found hitherto in the necessity of providing a sufficient inducement to save. But we have shown that the extent of effective saving is necessarily determined by the scale of investment and that the scale of investment is promoted by a low rate of interest ... Thus it is to our best advantage to reduce the rate of interest to that point relatively to the schedule of the marginal efficiency of capital at which there is full employment.[7]

Under Keynesian economics, the interest rate is thus one of the main levers to achieving full employment. Lower interest rates are advocated for the benefit of the whole of society. In classical economic theory, however, the interest rate is not seen as a policy tool but remains the domain of the individual creditor and debtor. But, despite laissez-faire theory, the interest rate did acquire a steering function in liberal systems as well. 'It is fairly clear, however, that this [classical] tradition has regarded the rate of interest as the factor which brings the demand for investment and the willingness to save into equilibrium with each other.'[8] Keynes not only finds this notion erroneous, but considers failure to use the interest rate as a political tool actually negligent, given the obligation incumbent upon the state to serve a common good.

> But the notion that the rate of interest is the balancing factor which brings the demand for saving in the shape of new investment forthcoming at a given rate of interest into equality with the supply of saving which results at that rate of interest from the community's psychological propensity to save, breaks down as soon as we perceive that

it is impossible to deduce the rate of interest merely from a knowledge of these two factors.[9]

Keynes thus found classical economic theory to be at fault in its analysis of the economy, lacking in the way classical liberals used tools, such as the interest rate, and grossly negligent of the well-being of the people.

The other important determinant of equilibrium is the quantity of money. The logical link between interest rates and quantity of money is scarcity: 'The owner of capital can obtain interest because capital is scarce, just as the owner of land can obtain rent because land is scarce. But whilst there may be intrinsic reason for the scarcity of land, there are no intrinsic reasons for the scarcity of money.'[10] Therefore, the state can use the amount of money in circulation to spur on the economy:

> Thus, if there is perfectly elastic supply so long as there is unemployment, and perfectly inelastic supply so soon as full employment is reached, and if effective demand changes in the same proportion as the quantity of money, the Quantity Theory of Money can be enunciated as follows: 'So long as there is unemployment, employment will change in the same proportion as the quantity of money; and when there is full employment, prices will change in the same proportion as the quantity of money'.[11]

The aim for Keynes, again, is to achieve full employment. To that end he suggests that the quantity of money be adapted accordingly, which effectively means 'printing money' to stimulate the economy, or what is today called quantitative easing. But Keynes goes even further, saying that such a policy could avoid speculation – which was rampant in the 1920s and '30s, turning investing into gambling and the stock exchanges into casinos. Neither served the common good; both tended to inhibit the proper working of the real economy:

> This we might aim … at an increase in the volume of capital until it ceases to be scarce, so that the functionless investor will no longer receive a bonus; and at a scheme of direct taxation which allows the intelligence and determination and executive skill of the financier, the entrepreneur … to be harnessed to the service of the community on reasonable terms of reward.[12]

Investment in stocks by real entrepreneurs was, accordingly, in the interests of society, because it would create added value and employment. Keynes saw speculation, or what he calls the 'functionless investor', as a perversion of market logic into pure profiteering without any benefit, that is, money for money's sake. This of course goes well beyond the development of economic theory and moves into the realm of ethics, a route not all classical liberals would wish to follow. But this is also to say that economic theory, even classical liberalism, has a moral basis, and classical liberals and Keynesians alike developed their theories accordingly. We have seen a good example of this already, in Hayek's liberalism. Thus economic theory has, as the cases looked at in this book have shown, always been a *social* theory, too. Economic theory not only describes society, but explores ideas of an ideal society. This is as good a definition as any of a moral cause, which we have seen here in liberalism, too – and that is of course exactly what Keynes was engaged in when he wrote his *General Theory*.

However, Keynes saw classical liberalism to be very much at fault, not so much because it advocated deficient policy but rather because of its passivity and insufficient awareness of important elements in the economic equation, notably the income level, which influences consumption and therefore economic growth.

> If the rate of interest is given as well as the demand curve for capital and the influence of the rate of interest on the readiness to save out of given levels of income, the level of

income must be the factor which brings the amount saved to equality with the amount invested. But in fact, the classical theory not merely neglects the influence of changes in the level of income, but involves formal error.

. . .

and there is no ground for supposing it to hold even in the long-period. In truth, the classical theory has not been alive to the relevance of changes in the level of income or to the possibility of the level of income being actually a function of the rate of the investment.[13]

Keynes gives several examples of where classical theory flies in the face of common sense and ignores the experience of real life:

If, indeed, it were true that the existing real wage is a minimum below which more labor than is now employed will not be forthcoming in any circumstances, involuntary unemployment, apart from frictional unemployment, would be non-existent. But to suppose that this is invariably the case would be absurd. For more labor than is at present employed is usually available for the existing money-wage.[14]

Applying the classical theory to a period of economic slump, as in the 1930s, did not work either.

A fall in real wages due to a rise in prices, with money-wages unaltered, does not, as a rule, cause the supply of available labor on offer at the current wage to fall below the amount actually employed prior to the rise of prices. To suppose that it does is to suppose that all those who are now unemployed though willing to work at the current wage will withdraw the offer of their labor in the event of even a small rise in the cost of living. Yet this strange supposition apparently underlies Professor Pigou's Theory of Unemployment, and it is what all members of the orthodox school are tacitly assuming.[15]

Keynes's remedy for the shortcomings of the classical theory is the proper use of the available economic tools, as elaborated in his *General Theory*:

> Thus the functions used by the classical theory, namely, the response of investment and the response of the amount saved out of a given income to change in the rate of interest, do not furnish material for a theory of the rate of interest; but they could be used to tell us what the level of income will be, given (from some other sources) the rate of interest; and, alternatively, what the rate of interest will have to be, if the level of income is to be maintained at a given figure (e.g. the level corresponding to full employment).[16]

Keynes argued that the rate of interest could and should be manipulated, using existing economic tools, so as to achieve stable income at full employment. But that was not what classical economists did with their economic theories – rather the opposite, as we have seen. Keynes had proved that the classical theory worked properly only in a situation of full employment, a situation in which there was no 'involuntary unemployment'.[17] Thus Keynes concluded, 'We need to throw over the second postulate of the classical doctrine and to work out the behaviour of a system in which involuntary unemployment in the strict sense is possible.'[18] Unemployment reflected the reality in which Keynes was living, that is, millions of unemployed willing but unable to find work. Keynes's theory is thus as much a wake-up call to classical liberal economists – exposing the fact that their teachings did not reflect reality – as it is a new interpretation of the functions of the economy for a society.

What is interesting to note is that although the *General Theory* is mostly presented as an economic theory, there is also an element of wrath in it against the 'functionless investor' (as we have seen). The functionless investor defends his often speculative profits with arguments of classical economic theory, while denying social justice to the worker. Rampant unemployment was the disastrous consequence of such immoral behaviour, which led Keynes to appeal to the 'honest entrepreneur', who would make a profit out of his economic activity but not fall prey to the fallacious logic of hitting the workers even harder with wage cuts. Keynes gave good economic reasons in support of behaviour that would be more beneficial both to the entrepreneur and to workers:

> Perhaps it will help to rebut the crude conclusion that a reduction in money-wages will increase employment 'because it reduces the cost of production', if we follow up the course of events on the hypothesis most favourable to this view, namely that at the outset entrepreneurs expect the reduction in money-wage to have this effect. It is indeed not unlikely that the individual entrepreneur, seeing his own costs reduced, will overlook at the outset the repercussions on the demand for his product and will act on the assumption that he will be able to sell at a profit a larger output than before. If, then, the entrepreneurs generally act on this expectation, will they in fact succeed in increasing their profits? Only if the community's marginal propensity to consume is equal to unity, so that there is no gap between the increment of income and the increment of consumption; or if there is an increase in investment corresponding to the gap between the increment of income and the increment of consumption, which will only occur if the schedule of marginal efficiencies of capital has increased relatively to the rate of interest . . . Thus the proceeds realized from the increased output will disappoint the entrepreneur and employment will fall back again to its previous figure . . . At the best, the date of their disappointment can only be

delayed for the interval during which their own investment
in increased working capital is filling the gap.[19]

So rather than cutting actual wages one could concede a modest
degree of inflation or impose indirect taxation, if real wages need
to be reduced. This was politically more acceptable and economically more sensible.[20] It corresponds to what we see today in the
general increase of value-added tax, rather than directly taxing
wages. But here our field is once again government policy rather
than individual entrepreneurial activity; this became another way
for Keynes to argue that state intervention is necessary in any case
and, this being so, had better be implemented properly – with the
state setting the economic framework in interest rates, quantity of
money and its own investment, if necessary. 'Thus apart from the
necessity of central controls to bring about an adjustment between
the propensity to consume and the inducement to invest, there is
no more reason to socialize economic life than there was before.'[21]
This became the framework of Roosevelt's New Deal in the 1930s
in the United States.

For Hayek, such 'planning' was one of the key postulates of
socialism. Seductively neutral, it was clearly a socialist policy, which,
he does not deny, was meant at its root to improve the lives of ordinary people. John Maynard Keynes, though no socialist, took up this
tenet of socialism, turned it into a viable economic theory and made
it the dominant economic doctrine of the 1930s, and on into the
mid-1970s, still having major repercussions in economic policies right
up to the financial crisis of 2008. For Hayek, however, economic
planning must lead inevitably to authoritarian and even totalitarian
politics, according to which the citizens' life is ultimately planned,
into the very nooks and crannies of his day-to-day existence. Hence
the title of his remarkable book *The Road to Serfdom* – a road which
must eventually lead to the destruction of civilization.[22]

It was unfortunate for Hayek, working as he was between the
London School of Economics and Cambridge, that the academic

current of the time flowed very much against his own ideas. Economics was absorbed by war planning and followed (it so happened) Keynes and the realization of his ideas of economic planning, which had been implemented under the New Deal to what many considered spectacular effect.[23] The views of the two men on the economy are, in many respects, diametrically opposed. Where Keynes seeks full employment, Hayek said that 'to aim always at the maximum of employment achievable by monetary means is a policy which is certain in the end to defeat its own purpose.'[24] Where Keynes calls for an active and indeed dominant economic policy on the part of the state, Hayek saw only the thin end of a sinister totalitarian wedge.[25]

> Although the state controls directly the use of only a large part of the available resources, the effects of its decisions on the remaining part of the economic system become so great that indirectly it controls almost everything. Where, as was, for example, true in Germany as early as 1928, the central and local authorities directly control the use of more than half of the national income (according to an official German estimate then, 53 per cent), they control indirectly almost the whole economic life of the nation. There is, then, scarcely an individual end which is not dependent for its achievement on the action of the state.[26]

However, that was exactly – or, at any rate, to an unprecedented degree – what Keynesians were implementing in the USA: that is, dominant state interference in the economy, not least, of course, in order to win the war, when it came.[27] Keynes also held that a substantial proportion of economic activity must be initiated by the state if the common purpose is to be achieved – be that full employment or the defeat of Nazi Germany.

Where Keynes urges massive anti-cyclical state investment to avoid the worst malfunctions of the market economy – for example, the Great Depression – Hayek advocated laissez-faire liberalism in order to preserve freedom in the most general of its meanings.[28] His example of choice is the preservation of parliamentary democracy in times of a war economy:

> It is important clearly to see the causes of this admitted ineffectiveness of parliaments when it comes to a detailed administration of the economic affairs of a nation. The fault is neither with the individual representatives nor with parliamentary institutions as such, but with the contradictions inherent in the task with which they are charged. They are not asked to act where they can agree, but to produce agreement on everything – the whole direction of the resources of the nation. For such a task the system of majority decision is, however, not suited. Majorities will be found where it is a choice between limited alternatives ... A democratic assembly voting and amending a comprehensive economic plan clause by clause, as it deliberates on an ordinary bill, makes nonsense. An economic plan, to deserve the name, must have a unitary conception. Even if parliament could, proceeding step by step, agree some scheme, it would certainly in the end satisfy nobody. A complex whole where all the parts must be most carefully adjusted to each other cannot be achieved through a compromise between conflicting views. To draw up an economic plan in this fashion is even less possible than, for example, successfully to plan a military campaign by democratic procedure. As in strategy it would become inevitable to delegate the task to the experts.[29]

The danger, for Hayek, is obvious. Such experts are bound to build up their own fiefdoms and could well end up as another Hitler or Stalin.[30] Almost in a functionalist manner, Hayek sees the demise of democracy as sooner or later inevitable once economic planning is introduced.[31]

Democratic government has worked successfully where, and so long as, the functions of government were, by a widely accepted creed, restricted to fields where agreement among a majority could be achieved by free discussion; and it is the great merit of the liberal creed that it reduced the range of subjects on which agreement was necessary to one on which it was likely to exist in a society of free men. It is now often said that democracy will not tolerate 'capitalism'. If 'capitalism' means here a competitive system based on free disposal over private property, it is far more important to realise that only within this system is democracy possible. When it becomes dominated by a collectivist creed, democracy will inevitably destroy itself.[32]

Why is democracy so important? Hayek asks intriguingly, almost provokingly. His answer: because it guarantees internal peace and individual freedoms.[33] Planning (of the type Keynes was suggesting) cannot do that. And that is why it is bound to fail, according to Hayek. It is the demands of economic planning, involving the totality of society, that are diametrically opposed to the limitation of power in a democracy. It is precisely this limitation of power, the inbuilt conflict of interests, checks and balances, and eventually the accountability of every minister before parliament that preserve Western liberal democracy as we know it.[34] Here, Hayek's message rings true.

5

Man is *Not* the Master
of His Own Fate:
Misguided Socialist Idealism

Hayek strays from the path of reason when he continues his defence of liberalism through the sharp criticism of socialism, which he sees as at best a *misguided* idealism:[1]

> the belief that Socialism would bring freedom is genuine and sincere. But this would only heighten the tragedy if it should prove that what was promised to us as the Road to Freedom was in fact the High Road to Serfdom.[2]

Socialism emphasizes the equality of individuals and argues that everyone should have equal opportunity to pursue their own happiness. The liberalism which Hayek describes as the ideal state of affairs, however, gives priority to those who take the initiative for their own interests. They do not need such postulates of equality, because they are able to make a living for themselves. Hayek does not go as far as those classical liberals such as Edmund Burke who claimed that equality will destroy society:

> perfect equality ... that is to say, equal want, equal wretchedness, equal beggary, and on the part of the partitioners [of their wealth] a woeful, helpless, and desperate disappointment. Such is the event of all compulsory equalizations. They pull down what is above. They never raise what is

below: and they depress high and low together beneath
the level of what was originally the lowest.[3]

For Hayek, too, however, the main flaw in the socialist postulate
of equality is that it starts out from the need to ensure the protection
of the weak in society.[4] Hayek does not acknowledge the inherent flaw
in the free market economy – namely, that those who already have
at their disposal sufficient resources (natural or material) will always
have better prospects of enrichment, whether they be workaholics or
bone idle. Being born into affluence is often enough to ensure greater
'success' in life than will ever be vouchsafed for the most intelligent
and industrious poor child – and nor does the injustice stop there.
Such perceived, often flagrant, unfairness is perhaps the most important source of the socialist movement and has been invoked in many
of its writings (Karl Marx's *Das Kapital* is the prime example where
this feeling of social injustice can be felt).[5] Like liberalism itself, it
came into being as a counter-movement, in this case to liberalism
taken too far.[6] The trades union movements of the nineteenth century
sprang up as a protest against unrestrained exploitation, poverty and
hardship in industrial heartlands, such as prevailed in Manchester,
or Essen in the Ruhr. Here, underprivileged workers tried to take
control of their own lives, leading to the socialist belief that man can
and should change his own fate. The creation of a just, or at any rate
less blatantly *un*just, society became the ultimate aim.

Classical liberal theory offered no answer to these important
observations. Life, for thinkers such as Adam Smith, had always
been a struggle. Life was *not* fair. There had never been any genuine
equality of opportunity.[7] Hayek does not stray far from this tenet
of liberalism when he says that freedom from want, or a guaranteed
minimum standard of living – a contemporary socialist demand –
was not a reasonable policy objective:[8]

To the great apostles of political freedom the word had
meant freedom from coercion, freedom from the arbitrary

power of other men, release from the ties which left the individual no choice but obedience to the orders of a superior to whom he was attached. The new freedom promised [by socialists], however, was to be freedom from necessity, release from the compulsion of the circumstances which inevitably limit the range of choice of all of us, although for some very much more than for others. Before man could be truly free, the 'despotism of physical want' had to be broken, the 'restraints of the economic system' relaxed. Freedom in this sense is, of course, merely another name for power or wealth. Yet, although the promises of this new freedom were often coupled with irresponsible promises of a great increase in material wealth in a socialist society, it was not from such an absolute conquest of the niggardliness of nature that economic freedom was expected. What the promise really amounted to was that the great existing disparities in the range of choice of different people were to disappear. The demand for the new freedom was thus only another name for the old demand for an equal distribution of wealth.[9]

Classical liberals even went so far as to say that governments should not try to change a state of affairs in which there was poverty, suffering and hunger, such as in Ireland during the Great Famine. The reasons given were that, on the one hand, such efforts to eradicate poverty could not succeed, and on the other, the free market needed masses of poor workers, just like any other commodity under the supply-and-demand logic, as Edmund Burke stressed: 'Labour is a commodity like every other, and rises or falls according to demand.'[10]

One must pose the critical question here as to what is the lesser evil: to try to remedy the hardships of people and try to achieve a better world, however idealist or utopian the aspiration? Or not to try at all, and let the market forces – which evidently did not provide a solution to the poverty of the time – run their course? Here Hayek is in fact a little more moderate than some of his liberal forebears:

security against severe physical privation, the certainty of a given minimum of sustenance for all ... There is no reason why in a society that has reached the general level of wealth which ours has attained, [this] kind of security should not be guaranteed to all without endangering general freedom.[11]

However, in the best liberal tradition, he stresses that wealth has first to be created, and here, in the general debate, argues that too much attention was given to those in need, rather than considering how the productive forces in society can be stimulated and better harnessed to the right goals:

According to the views now dominant the question is no longer how we can make the best use of the spontaneous forces found in a free society. We have in effect undertaken to dispense with the forces which produced unforeseen results and to replace the impersonal and anonymous mechanism of the market by collective and 'conscious' direction of all social forces to deliberately chosen goals.[12]

Hayek closes the circle to his liberal forebears when he says that there has not yet been a workable plan to eradicate poverty.[13]

However, this is where socialists protest, driven by the actual experience of poverty. Their challenge comes in a simple reversal of priorities. The economy should serve men and not the other way around. For Hayek this is the beginning of all evils, because effectively this turns the economic rationale on its head. From his perspective, the question is no longer what price one can achieve for a product, but how much the worker who produces it wants to be paid. Hayek's supposition of a negative disposition inherent in human nature – which marks him as rather more conservative than liberal, although in liberal economics both conservatism and liberalism often go well together – leads to the obvious conclusion that wages will rise relentlessly and exorbitantly.[14] Personal greed would drive a wage spiral. Organizations were put in place to enforce such interests, for example, trades unions in the workplace and on the streets, and socialist parties in politics.

For Hayek, this is the making of a vicious circle. Sooner or later, moderate socialists will be replaced by revolutionary communists or fascists.[15] For him, their roots are the same: '*Balilla* and *Hitlerjugend*, *Dopolavoro* and *Kraft durch Freude*, political uniforms and military party formations, are all little more than imitations of older socialist institutions.'[16] The inherent tendency, discerned by Hayek, for socialism to embrace radicalization would consume the moderate and benign founding fathers of socialism by a process comparable with that described by Burke – no admirer of the French Revolution – that is, a process of radicalization whereby the revolution ultimately devours its own children.[17] For Hayek, this process can only lead sooner or later to dictatorship – not of the proletariat, as Karl Marx claimed, but a dictatorship by the worst and most radical communists, whom Hayek considered the worst breed of mankind.

Finally, he admits that the market cannot solve everything, such as the problem of dire poverty, but claims that it offers by far the best overall solution, because liberalism is not just market liberalism but also safeguards political and private freedoms and general liberty – which would be lost under a communist or collectivist dictatorship.[18]

Keynes would probably subscribe to Hayek's description of the merits of the liberal market economy, but, though himself no socialist, he would also subscribe to the socialist ideal of justice in society and the idea that man must make at least some effort to improve the lot of his less fortunate fellow citizens. For Keynes, this endeavour falls squarely on the state, which has an obligation to guide the economy so that it can provide for its citizens. Keynes started his criticism of classical liberal economic theory at the suboptimal functioning of the market: 'The outstanding faults of the economic society in which we live are its failure to provide for full employment and its arbitrary and inequitable distribution of wealth and incomes.'[19] This comes very close to a socialist analysis and even has common ground with aspects of Marxist analyses. He goes further in the moral cause, saying that for very human reasons, such as family, language or culture, there has always been 'imperfect mobility of labor'.[20] This is the first reason why men cannot be treated as just another commodity under the supply-and-demand logic of the market economy, and this ties in very much with socialist and Marxist reasoning.[21] What was wrong with the market logic was that the employer   makes a profit and the worker becomes merely a tool exploited in the process. In classical liberal logic, this has been justified as follows:

> I premise that labour is, as I have already intimated, a commodity, and as such, an article of trade ... When any commodity is carried to the market, it is not the necessity of the vendor, but the necessity of the purchaser that raises the price. The extreme want of the seller has rather (by the nature of things with which we shall in vain contend) the direct contrary operation. If the goods at market are beyond the demand, they fall in their value; if below it, they rise. The impossibility of the subsistence of a man, who carries his labour to a market, is totally beside the question in this way of viewing it. The only question is, what is it worth to the buyer?[22]

The consequences of this process are captured in Marx's concept of alienation.[23] 'The potential harshness of that relationship can be mitigated by labor market regulation, but the essential "thing-ification" of wage-labor remains.'[24] This names the fundamental moral problem of the free market under an industrial logic, in that it disconnects work from the worker. It takes away the special act of creation from the craftsman, an act which is based on a choice to make something and may well be seen as a definition of humanity. Renouncing actual creativity in order to make a living happens later. When work is defined as a good like any other, it makes of the worker a mere machine, no longer a human being. The threat of poverty deprived the worker in industrialized societies of the choice as regards the destination of the fruits of his labour. Effectively, this reinforces the dehumanization of work, on which Marx then based his concept of alienation.[25]

Keynes does not espouse a Marxist rationale feeding into the trades union and later the socialist movements, but he shares the abstract tenet of socialist policy objectives firmly rejected by every liberal economist in the 1920s and '30s, that is, socialization or nationalization: 'a somewhat comprehensive socialization of investment will prove the only means of securing an approximation to full employment.'[26] That was what was happening in authoritarian and totalitarian regimes, the USSR being the one ideologically most feared in Britain in Keynes's earlier period. However, Keynes moderates his argument:

> It is not the ownership of the instruments of production [a Marxist claim] which it is important for the state to assume. If the state is able to determine the aggregate amount of resources devoted to augmenting the instruments and the basic rate of reward to those who own them, it will have accomplished all that is necessary. Moreover, the necessary measures of socialisation can be introduced gradually and without a break in the general traditions of society.[27]

This is really a dividing point vis-à-vis Marxist analysis, which proclaims that the state should become the owner of all the means of production, so that ultimately the working class is in command of these tools, first through the state itself, and then through the avant-gardist communist party. Marx predicted that ultimately the state will then 'wither away'.[28]

In the post-war period, the issue of nationalization was one of the classic conflicts between capital and labour. Germany can serve as an example. The conservatives (Christian Democratic Union) emphasized the traditional criticisms of undemocratic technocracy and the highly bureaucratic command economy.[29] The Social Democratic Party (SPD) – constitutional Marxists much further to the left than they are today – countered:

> the key industries and the primary sector must be nationalised. This is because where democracy is understood as the right of people to determine its own destiny, power in the economy cannot be allowed to lie with groupings, which can evade proper democratic control through their economic strength.[30]

In the socialist credo, permanent control of economic power would make government intervention necessary only in times of crisis, because problems could be solved from the very outset. Controlled economies, which could undoubtedly deal much better with times of crisis than a muddled liberal democracy, would also prevent regression into totalitarian regimes. In addition, the complexity of the modern economy seemed to demand central planning. All these were reasons to lead the SPD to argue for a command economy in West Germany in the post-war period. The ideal was to bring economic competition in line with the needs of the people.[31] Only with the Godesberg programme of 1959 was the SPD concept of the command economy substantially adapted.[32] From then on, the SPD opted for the idea of an economy planned along Keynesian lines, an approach informing economic policy in the early years of the first post-war SPD government under Willy Brandt, importantly accepting enforced competition among firms as the driving force in the economy, but moderated by economic planning and redistributive policies.[33] Therefore, at the macroeconomic level, the SPD was very much in favour of an active economic policy of the Keynesian type, using public investment as an economic stimulus. Economic stability was most important, not least because of the social and individual repercussions of unemployment.[34]

Keynes did not believe that all means of production – or even only the 'commanding heights of the economy' – should be nationalized, but central economic planning for the purpose of achieving full employment he took to be fundamental. At this juncture, one may have to ask what kind of employment Keynesian politics would produce. Would it be productive employment, as Keynes would suggest, or would it be 'job creation' (as deplored by Hayek) under a command economy, as in the USSR? The latter, with the benefit of hindsight, seems hardly desirable, because it is unproductive and it was one major reason why the Soviet economy was worn down. Nowadays, economic discussions around this topic centre on the issue of an unconditional minimum income, or indeed unemployment benefits and social support.[35] Some have called this 'socialism after Hayek':

> The solution to the 'thingification' problem is not to replace a capitalist employer with a public employer, but to institute universal self-employment . . . real-world financial markets often deny credit to those who lack sufficient collateral, i.e. the typical worker. Consequently, to facilitate a robust self-employment system probably requires some sort of wealth redistribution program, for instance, government provisions of universal capital grants. These are the practical messages of *Socialism after Hayek*: strive for labor appropriation and wealth redistribution; let private property and market exchange remain.[36]

This lends some credit to a variety of social business concepts, the central idea of which is probably as old as the market itself, and if classical liberal theory is right this means that both are as old as mankind. What unites them is really the opposition to the profit logic of the market. Marxists denounced the resulting perversions of exploitation and alienation.[37] Under the command economy, the USSR proclaimed the liberation of mankind through the abandonment of the profit rationale.[38] In the West, different models by which employees became shareholders in the companies they worked in – 'participation' – were tried out, to moderate, at least, the profit rationale and have employees enjoy some real share in a company's fruits: 'if capitalist firms make profit-sharing contracts with workers, the economy will be much less subject to demand shocks than if capitalist firms use typical wage-for-labor contracts.'[39] And one can even go as far as to suggest that the state should make available funds for an employer of last resort, who engages in non-profitable, but nevertheless useful, services:

> Might not the state directly promote the capability to work through some employer-of-last-resort scheme? . . . state funding for non-profit organizations that hire the unemployed to engage in projects of civic improvement not generally undertaken by profit-seeking enterprises.[40]

As a policy, Hayek, ever the pessimist, would clearly see this as a precursor to the Nazi Labour Service (Arbeitsdienst), which can only result in social misery and which is always open to abuse, as indeed occurred under totalitarian regimes.

What is interesting, however, in these social business initiatives, is that the merits of the entrepreneurial spirit have been accepted. The concept of profit as a motivation is not contested, but rather the idea of profit *maximization*. Such business concepts have been known for a long time in commercial non-profit organizations, which instead of resorting to traditional charitable practices charge a fee to customers without the intention to maximize profits. As non-profit organizations they are legally banned, in many countries, from distributing dividends. Decisions to move on from charity in the pure form to embrace commercial strategies have been identified as a major change in the way the third sector operates.[41] Commercial strategy in this context means the creation of a new form of organization that lies in between for-profit business and non-profit organizations and that could be defined more precisely as non-loss, non-divided firms pursuing social goals.[42]

The idea of establishing by statute a basic income for all has also been mooted in recent years in the context of achieving a more just, free and even more effective society. The concept of the basic income comes from the claim that the current administration of welfare and unemployment benefits, the means testing required (and often hated) and the fairness such a redistributive system must serve could well cost more than simply paying every citizen a lump sum regardless of his or her situation.[43] After that, the citizen decides for him- or herself what activity to pursue. This idea advocates the effective decoupling of the need to earn a living from the joy that productive work can provide. Part of the case for a basic income of this kind is that Western industrialized societies are rich enough to provide one to all their members. Huge improvements in productivity won through mechanization, rationalization and computerization have transformed the original battle, in which so many fought to eke out a minimal existence, into a problem of redistributing abundant or at least ample wealth – largely created by machines – to all members of society.[44] This means that human creativity rather than the obligation to earn a wage could become the centre of the world of work.

To some extent, this is already happening through the widespread institution of the minimum wage, which can only be guaranteed because of mechanized added value and resulting higher productivity. The question which naturally comes up at this point is, why should anyone work at all, if a basic income is handed out to everyone? The answer that advocates of a basic income give is: because people will *want* to work:

> A basic income policy would avoid the knowledge problem that government officials face in trying to implement welfare policies that are targeted specifically to enhance individuals' unique capabilities deficiencies . . . labor becomes 'life's prime want' . . . the non-monetary attractiveness of labor . . .

pleasant work and leisure as much as possible. If the second option is preferable, then we might want to combine a universal basic income grant with universal self-employment.[45]

This posits the – somewhat extravagant – argument that it is work which gives sense to the individual's life. The resulting benefits of productive work could be added to a basic income. Employers would have to offer interesting, attractive and meaningful work. Employers would also be freer in their entrepreneurial activities. Their social obligations towards employees would disappear, and the employee would always have the option to leave, if they found the work to be unsatisfactory. There would be no hardship, because the employee would be covered by the basic income. 'Hire and fire' management techniques would be less objectionable, because they would no longer carry with them the menace of poverty. This would, to put it mildly, constitute a revolutionary change of the economic system.[46] It also sounds like a utopian society very different from the free market economy we have today.

However, would things really radically change? The relative power positions of employer and employee would remain the same, with poverty remaining a relative concept. One can argue that an employee can always leave their job without fear of hardship, but despite the fact that their basic necessities would be covered by their basic income and provided by the state, this employee could still be in relative poverty as compared with those who remain in employment. In addition, the question of the control of economic power is important. If market logic prevails, importantly with fewer controls on social or fair practices, the gap between rich and poor could well yawn ever wider. Would society accept this and could a state, which is inevitably weaker under that concept, control the economic power of the rich? Such a situation could pose serious problems for the balance of power in a democracy. In addition, work, however satisfying, is by its very nature not always pleasant. What happens to the work no one wants to do? Could we really leave all such work to machines, and would that not mean more alienation from the production processes on which our societies are based? The basic income remains, as shown in these questions, a very idealistic theory; it might make sense in economic terms, but there remain serious questions regarding power relations and the impact on the structure of society as a whole. This seems to suggest that the 'basic income' concept has all the makings of an economic theory, but woefully lacks the important part, where an economic theory becomes a social theory, explaining in a comprehensive manner how society should work.

Let us come back to Keynes's *General Theory*. He provided such an explanation of how society should work in suggesting that the malfunctioning of the market economy could be remedied by macroeconomic planning and 'steering':

> Our criticism of the accepted classical theory of economics has consisted not so much in finding logical flaws in its analysis as in pointing out that its tacit assumptions are seldom or never satisfied, with the result that it cannot solve the economic problems of the actual world. But if our central control succeeds in establishing an aggregate volume of output corresponding to full employment as nearly as is practicable, the classical theory comes into its own again from this point onwards. If we suppose the volume of output to be given, i.e. to be determined by forces outside the classical scheme of thought, then there is no objection to be raised against the classical analysis of the manner in which private self-interest will determine what in particular is produced, in what proportion the factors of production will be combined to produce it, and how the value of the final product will be distributed between them.[47]

This sounds very promising, but this Keynesian economic logic came to grief as times changed, when, particularly in the 1960s and

'70s, governments, such as that of social democrat Willy Brandt in Germany and, later, the socialist government of François Mitterrand in France, abandoned central planning of the economy, because it created more market distortion than it yielded economic benefits. In general, the idea that the centrally planned output has to correspond to full employment and that the state would set the framework so that this level of output can be reached is fine in theory. However, the liberal criticism of Keynesian economics had always been that in reality the state will either use a specific set of companies, for example state-owned companies such as Électricité de France or Renault, to invest directly, or use powers available to it to stimulate the market indirectly via interest rates and monetary policy. In both cases the danger is that the market will anticipate state action:

> If Government makes all its purchases at once, it will instantly raise the market upon itself. If it makes them by degrees, it must follow the course of the market. If it follows the course of the market, it will produce no effect, and the consumer may as well buy as he wants – therefore all the expense is incurred gratis.[48]

Entrepreneurs will try to make the most profit out of such a situation and this normally results in market distortion. Eventually, there was strong evidence in Germany and France of the 1970s and '80s, for example, that market activity cannot be confined to the inside of what Keynes would consider the framework the state sets to achieve a certain level of output corresponding to full employment.

6

Liberal Polemic, or, the Threat of National Socialism

From Hayek's perspective, the political consequences for society of planning the economy were worse than the predicted economic repercussions outlined in the previous chapter. As we saw earlier in this book, liberalism has always had two roots in economic and civil freedoms, which are both seen as fundamentally indispensable to the concept of the 'good society'. In contrast, extreme nationalism, as under the Nazis in Germany, and economic planning as practised in the Soviet Union, were movements diametrically opposed to citizens' enjoyment of their vital freedoms. For Hayek, these systems embodied attitudes utterly destructive to any freedom, which was what liberals like him would consider as the right way for humans to live in the good society. In this statement, clearly revealed already in his *Road to Serfdom*, the roots of the development of totalitarianism as a theory are exposed. After the war, Hayek became the key driver in the development of the theory which postulates the link between Nazi Germany and the Soviet Union in their totalitarian aspirations.

This development of totalitarianism as a theory underpinning the Cold War will be discussed in this chapter. In a cruder version, however, it existed already during the Second World War, in the formula: nationalism + socialism = National Socialism. Popular in conservative circles, the formula led some to forget the conservative appeasement policy of the Chamberlain period. It became a rallying cry in the Cold War in the confrontation between the Western bloc and the Soviet Union, which could then be conceived as just the same old enemy – yet another totalitarian regime. It also gave the West the confidence to fight out to the end the Cold War against the Soviet Union, because liberal democracies had already triumphed over the totalitarian Nazi regime. However, beyond this use of the theory of totalitarianism, which was somewhat distorted at best, there were some deeper truths that the history of two world wars had revealed. One of them was that loyalty to the nation had been convincingly shown to be more important than class affiliation. The Socialist International had broken down on the eve of the First World War. The national paradigm prevailed and the ideal of a unification of the working class across national boundaries was not dead, but in the First World War, when the question was brutally posed, it became clear that workers, in times of crisis, were not prepared to abandon ancient and deep-rooted loyalties to their countries and their leaderships. They fought in their respective national armies and the socialist rationale of loyalty to class was found to be weaker than patriotism.

In the environment of national politics, socialists had always been accused, in right-wing conservative circles, of lacking love of country. This became a particularly pertinent criticism when, during the interwar years, socialist parties became strong enough to form governments, as was the case in most of Western Europe. Socialist overcompensation becomes obvious in the immediate post-war years. The British Labour Party and the German SPD constitute striking examples of socialist parties pursuing strongly nationalistic policies, often even more enthusiastically than their right-wing conservative competitors. The Conservatives in Britain and the Christian Democratic Union (CDU) in Germany were much keener on European integration policies after the Second World War than the left-wing parties. The following quotation from the leading French trade unionist Léon Jouhaux, from a speech made at the first congress of the International Federation of Trade Unions in London in 1950, illustrates this decisive moment for the Labour movement:

What seems to me the first aim, the first objective, the first goal, of our new organization is peace. This is not a new problem. The working classes and the trade unions have always desired peace, but if we ask ourselves honestly: 'Have we succeeded in getting peace?' we must have the courage to say that we did not succeed. It was because we did not act at the moment when we should have acted; because we did not speak at the moment when we should have spoken; because we have been influenced by the rising nationalism of every one of our countries; and because we have chosen the national answer instead of obeying the mandate of the International. Therefore, we have failed.[1]

In Hayek, one finds this sombre confession seen as an indictment of socialism in general. Invoking exactly the above argument, he discerned little more than hypocrisy in the socialist maintenance of the internationalist ideal.

In addition, socialism turning into communism posed a serious ideological threat to the maintenance of Western liberal democracies, such as that found in Great Britain: 'The war will bring about changes which may be fundamental and revolutionary in the economic and the social life of this country. On this we are all agreed.'[2] By 1943, when Hayek was writing, the fear that the war would break up the social consensus in Britain, which had had a coalition government since 1940, had been dispelled. Anthony Eden, at the Foreign Office, meant 'revolutionary' in the above quotation literally in the sense of a revolution of the working class fuelled by communist ideology. We may note in passing that this fear of revolution accounts in no small degree for appeasement tendencies towards fascism among British conservatives before the war, and for the geopolitical opposition to the Soviet Union. However, the war showed once again how love of country *can* prevail over considerations of class ideology. Britain did not fall apart along class lines, as Eden had feared, and the people, for the greater part, rallied to support their government during the war, regardless of class. This is the background to Hayek's emphasis on the hypocrisy between the internationalist ideal and the nationalist reality of socialist parties across Europe:

> That Socialism so long as it remains theoretical, is inter-nationalist, while as soon as it is put into practice, whether in Russia or in Germany, it becomes violently nationalist, is one of the reasons why 'liberal Socialism' as most people in the Western world imagine it is purely theoretical, while the practice of Socialism is everywhere totalitarian.[3]

This accusation led to the blunt formula of nationalism + socialism = National Socialism, a concept widely touted by conservatives in Britain, even, bewilderingly, by Winston Churchill.

Keynes, naturally, saw other forces at work. He saw the 'classical theory', as he called it, very much as an ideology in its own right, defining our perception of good and evil. Liberalism, as first described by Ricardo, became accepted as the 'good' and its opponents by the definition of liberal theory as wrong, in the best case, and evil in nature in the worst. Keynes outlines this development of the establishment of liberal ideology in the following passage in his *General Theory*:

> The idea that we can safely neglect the aggregate demand function is fundamental to the Ricardian economics, which underlie what we have been taught for more than a century. Malthus, indeed, had vehemently opposed Ricardo's doctrine that it was impossible for effective demand to be deficient; but vainly. For, since Malthus was unable to explain clearly (apart from an appeal to the facts of common observation) how and why effective demand could be deficient or excessive, he failed to furnish an alternative construction; and Ricardo conquered England as completely as the Holy Inquisition conquered Spain . . . the other point of view

completely disappeared; it ceased to be discussed. It could only live on furtively, below the surface, in the underworlds of Karl Marx, Silvio Gesell or Major Douglas.[4]

In 'the underworlds of Karl Marx', we have one of the few references made by Keynes to Marxist theory, and it is clearly a sympathetic one, regretting the neglect of some of the truths Marx pinpointed. Economically, this constituted an almost exclusive consideration of the supply side under liberal economics and a general neglect of the demand side. The common sense of the early trades union movement asked: who would buy the products workers were making, if all of them lived in poverty? Marxist theory and socialist political parties later developed out of this logic. Importantly, on this point Keynes clearly shares the socialist view when he argues that the 'right' side of the economic equation is the demand side. The main reasons he adduces are economic in nature, but the humanist aspiration that society ought to provide its citizens with opportunities for them to enjoy decent lives is equally important against the background of the utter failure of liberal market economies to do exactly that during the Great Depression. This became very clear in Keynes's assessment of the ability of the liberal market economy to tackle economic problems during the 1930s, when he was writing. 'It may well be that the classical theory represents the way in which we should like our economy to behave. But to assume that it actually does so is to assume our difficulties away.'[5] This failure of the liberal market economy during the Great Depression made Keynes ask how it could have come to this, where a failing economic model had become the dominant, if not the only, economic model:

> The completeness of the Ricardian victory is something of a curiosity and a mystery. It must have been due to a complex of suitabilities in the doctrine to the environment into which it was projected. That it reached conclusions quite different from what the ordinary uninstructed person would

expect, added, I suppose, to its intellectual prestige. That its teaching, translated into practice, was austere and often unpalatable, lent it virtue. That it was adapted to carry a vast and consistent logical superstructure, gave it beauty. That it could explain much social injustice and apparent cruelty as an inevitable incident in the scheme of progress, and the attempt to change such things as likely on the whole to do more harm than good, comm[e]nded it to authority. That it afforded a measure of justification to the free activities of the individual capitalist attracted to it the support of the dominant social force behind authority.[6]

Keynes's last point – that liberalism served the interest of the dominant social forces and went on doing so even during the Great Depression – is a striking counter-argument to Hayek's fear of socialism as leading to the loss of freedom. Keynes was in no doubt that it was the liberal market economy that had led inexorably to the Great Depression. Extreme economic nationalism in the imposition of tariffs and quotas was the consequence, externally. Internally, every economic freedom was nullified by resulting unemployment and poverty for unprecedented numbers of citizens.

Keynes worked his criticism of liberal economic theory into the development of his *General Theory*, postulating that it was the demand side of the economy that should bear the emphasis of economic policy. However, what that meant in reality was that ordinary workers ought to get a decent wage so that demand for the products they made was created. That would ease nationalism through economic means – very much what trade unions and socialists had advocated as common sense for over a century. Keynes was not daunted by attacks from conservative and liberal circles, which came as a logical consequence of the proximity of his *General Theory* to left-wing political agendas. He was convinced that the economic framework in which the free economy should work must be *planned*. To him it was clear that the laissez-faire policy of the liberal brand had led to disaster in the Great Depression, not to mention, if one went far back enough, the Irish Famine. Economic nationalism had arguably led to political dictatorships, such as in Nazi Germany and Soviet Russia. Planning the economic framework was, for Keynes, the way out of liberal market chaos and this was what was needed, if another Great Depression was to be avoided.

7

The Necessity of Planning

Keynes argued the case for planning by attacking the foundations of the free market economy, or what he called the 'classical theory'. He summarizes the foundations of the theory as follows:

> we have made the classical theory to depend in succession on the assumptions:
>
> 1. That the real wage is equal to the marginal disutility of the existing employment;
> 2. That there is no such thing as involuntary unemployment in the strict sense;
> 3. That supply creates its own demand in the sense that the aggregate demand price is equal to the aggregate supply price for all levels of output and employment.
>
> These three assumptions, however, all amount to the same thing in the sense that they all stand and fall together, any one of them logically involving the other two.[1]

The question Keynes then poses is whether these fundamental assumptions of free market economics hold true and whether they can fully explain the working of modern economies. He disagrees, saying that 'it is the part played by the aggregate demand function which has been overlooked.'[2]

So Keynes's answer is that the economic analysis of liberal economic theory is at best one-sided, if not definitely wrong. He argues that the economic logic must be inverted. It is not wages which must be lowered to produce more cheaply, but demand that must be stimulated, and this happens primarily if people have money to spend, earned from decently remunerated employment. In more technical terms, Keynes puts it as follows: 'expenditure on consumption in terms of the wage-unit depends in the main, on the volume of output and employment is the justification for summing up the other factors in the ... propensity to consume.'[3] Therefore, in order to increase employment towards full employment, the state must invest so that output levels correspond to full employment, or are close to it: 'employment can only increase *pari passu* with an increase in investment; unless, indeed, there is a change in the propensity to consume.'[4] From this conclusion, Keynes took his fundamental economic criticism against liberal economic theory:

> Thus the traditional analysis is faulty because it has failed to isolate correctly the independent variables of the system. Saving and investments are the determinates of the system, not the determinants. They are the twin results of the system's determinants, namely the propensity to consume, the schedule of the marginal efficiency of capital and the rate of interest.[5]

This means that the state must use the tools of the principal interest rate and, if necessary, investment programmes to achieve full employment. The social rationale, which is at the heart of Keynes's concerns, naturally, against the backdrop of the Great Depression, is that of achieving full employment for the good of society. He argues this by giving a striking example:

There are, of course, errors of foresight; but these would not be avoided by centralizing decisions. When 9,000,000 men are employed out of 10,000,000 willing and able to work, there is no evidence that the labor of these 9,000,000 men is miscredited. The complaint against the present system is not that these 9,000,000 men ought to be employed on different tasks, but that tasks should be available for the remaining 1,000,000 men. It is in determining the volume, not the direction, of actual employment that the existing system has broken down.[6]

Thus Keynes does not advocate the planning of the economy in detail, as practised by Soviet governments, where individual freedom of choice of occupation to all intents and purposes disappeared – Hayek's analysis rings all too true in relation to this type of 'command economy' planning. Keynes pleads for planning of the economic *framework*, which would provide the setting for free economic initiative inside the market. This means monetary and interest rate policies framed to create and maintain jobs, and state investment programmes to stimulate demand:

the result of filling in the gaps in the classical theory is not to dispose of the 'Manchester System', but to indicate the nature of the environment which the free play of economic forces requires if it is to realize the full potentialities of production. The central controls necessary to ensure full employment will, of course, involve a large extension of the traditional functions of government.[7]

Naturally, any liberal economist such as Hayek would strongly object to such state intervention in the market, because liberal economic theory argued that state intervention could not be confined merely to setting the framework, but must eventually encroach on individual freedoms, economic and civil. Keynes took up this criticism that his type of planning and the resulting 'enlargement of the functions of government . . . to be a terrific encroachment on individualism. I defend it, on the contrary, both as the only practicable means of avoiding the destruction of existing economic forms in their entirety and as the condition of the successful functioning of individual initiative.'[8] He goes on to argue that Keynesian economics will lead to much more sustainable and less volatile business activity:

> For if effective demand is deficient, not only is the public scandal of wasted resources intolerable, but the individual enterpriser who seeks to bring these resources into action is operating with the odds loaded against him . . . But if effective demand is adequate, average skill and average good fortune will be enough.[9]

The questions a liberal such as Hayek would critically pose here are whether government will have sufficient information to be in a position to decide accurately as to the output corresponding to full employment. Can such decisions be taken on a neutral basis or will they lead to corruption? Are democratic institutions strong enough to implement control mechanisms? Such very pertinent questions were posed with insistence at the time and they must still be posed today. The merit of Keynesian economics remains, however, in its moral aspiration. It is the well-being of human beings and human society that lie at the heart of Keynesian economics.[10] This comes very close to the socialist belief that the economy should serve men, not men the economy. Particularly after the Second World War, the main concern of socialists was the chaotic development of the economy in the immediate post-war years. Any return to the anarchic concepts of liberalism and free market economics, which were seen as one of the reasons for the war, was quite unacceptable.[11] It should be not the greed of the few but the needs of the many that are the driving rationale for economic decisions.[12] An intelligently planned economy would be a much more sensible way of organization, socialists argued.[13]

Beyond the variation of the interest rate for the purpose of creating jobs, and beyond state investment programmes, the nationalization of key industries – the 'commanding heights of the economy' – became a crucial socialist policy, particularly after the Second World War. Nationalization of the railways and heavy industry, for example, would bring key industries under state control, which would in turn enable the state to provide better for the needs of the people.[14] In addition, nationalization was seen as a method of enabling the ordinary worker to get involved in corporate management. Participatory rights became a key issue in this context: a way of ensuring proper boardroom representation of the workforce and of conferring on employees some power to pursue their own economic interests. Socialist doctrine argued that ultimately equilibrium would be achieved, which would help to foster a stable social fabric underpinning the formal structures of the state.

The German Social Democrats (SPD) serve, however, as a good example with which to illustrate the point that there were limits to the effectiveness of economic planning and the corresponding agenda of nationalization. At the macroeconomic level, the SPD was very much in favour of an active economic policy of the Keynesian type, using public investment as an economic stimulus. Economic stability was the priority, not least because of the social and individual repercussions of unemployment.[15] The ideal, again, was to bring economic competition in line with the needs of the people.[16] From 1959 onwards – we have already mentioned the Godesberg programme – the Keynesian concept of a planned economy, importantly accepting workable competition as the driving force and essential lubricant in the economy, moderated only by economic planning and redistributive schemes, became formal SPD policy.[17] This is what Western European social democrats finally came back to – largely what Keynes had proposed in his *General Theory*: a planned economy in which the state sets the framework of economic competition and leaves unfettered the market, with all its positive opportunities for private initiative and freedom to carry on with its good work.

Unfortunately, the separation of the external market framework and internal market workings was not that easy. This problem became one of the most plausible explanations for the failure of Keynesianism in the late 1970s – that the internal market *anticipated* the actions of the decision makers setting the economic framework. This led to market distortion rather than to market stimulation, and thus to inefficiencies, which were starkly exposed in the economic crisis following the oil shock of 1973.[18] In its aftermath, the attitude towards Keynesian economic planning changed. It became seen as having been part of the reason for the economic crises of the 1970s. The liberal position on planning of the economy was uncompromising, and Hayek became the leading – and formidable – theoretician of the fundamental opposition. Socialists intended planning to bring about more equality, or at any rate equality of opportunity: that at the very least those starting out in life should do so from positions of reasonable equality. Noble as this ideal might be, Hayek took the view that it was not in fact achievable. In this sense, his argument prepared the ground for the great ideological struggle of the post-war period in economic theory, which played out in free market doctrine versus socialist planning:[19]

The dispute between the modern planners and their opponents is, therefore, not a dispute on whether we ought to choose intelligently between the various possible organisations of society; it is not a dispute on whether we ought to employ foresight and systematic thinking in planning our common affairs. It is a dispute about what is the best way of so doing. The question is whether for this purpose it is better that the holder of coercive power should confine himself in general to creating conditions under which the knowledge and initiative of individuals is given the best scope so that they can plan most successfully; or whether a rational utilisation of our resources requires central direction and organisation of all our activities according to some consciously constructed 'blueprint'. The socialists of all parties have appropriated the term planning for planning of the latter type and it is now generally accepted in this sense. But though this is meant to suggest that this is the only rational way of handling our affairs, it does not of course prove this. It remains the point on which the planners and the liberals disagree.[20]

A good example might be the Iron and Steel Act of the Labour government as discussed in the House of Commons in 1950. Ideologically, the Conservative Party attacked the socialist paradigm of economic 'planability':

> that Act puts too much power in the hands of too few men who have too little knowledge. Even if they have the responsibility for the control of the whole industry, they have neither the knowledge nor the experience.[21]

Though taken from an ideological debate of the early 1950s, this sounds very much like the language of the classical liberals, such as John Stuart Mill, Adam Smith or Edmund Burke. Mill put it this way:

> but that a handful of human beings should weigh everybody in the balance, and give more to one and less to another at their sole pleasure and judgement, would not be borne unless from persons believed to be more than men, and backed by supernatural terrors.[22]

Adam Smith responded in a similar vein:

> The statesman, who should attempt to direct private people in what manner they ought to employ their capitals, would

not only load himself with a most unnecessary attention, but assume an authority which could safely be trusted to no council and senate whatever, and which would nowhere be so dangerous as in the hands of a man who had folly and presumption enough to fancy himself fit to exercise it.[23]

And Edmund Burke completes the circle of liberal classics on that point:

To provide for us in our necessities is not in the power of Government. It would be a vain presumption in statesmen to think they can do it. The people maintain them, and not they the people ... It is not only so of the state and statesman, but of all the classes and descriptions of the Rich – they are the pensioners of the poor, and are maintained by their superfluity. They are under the absolute, hereditary, and indefeasible dependance [sic] on those who labour, and are miscalled the Poor.[24]

Hayek went further. In contrast to such more benign interpretations, he believed that planning brought out the worst in men. He went beyond classical arguments of the invisible hand type, according to which the economy is simply too complex to be planned and there is a hidden logic of profit which produces the most beneficial outcomes for the whole of society.[25] Hayek borrowed from Jeremy Bentham's and J. S. Mill's utilitarianism the idea that the best policy is that which yields the greatest good for the greatest number.[26] Eventually, Hayek believed that planning must inexorably, in the medium to long term, lead to corruption and abuse of power.[27] Corruption will infect the small group of people who do the planning. But even worse, for those who are the objects of planning, no plan could ever be truly just.[28] Such a plan would require people to fulfil certain tasks – regardless of whether they wish to carry them out or not. It would determine the number of vacancies in all trades, callings, professions – regardless of the natural inclinations and abilities of people. It would require jobseekers to relocate to places where they were needed, regardless of family bonds, let alone free choice of their workplace.[29] It would determine the wage, regardless of quality of work, diligence or effort.[30] These are only a few examples used by Hayek to show that economic planning would sweep away all freedoms and eventually men's ability to determine or even only influence the course of their lives.[31] 'Hence the familiar fact that the more the state "plans" the more difficult planning becomes for the individual.'[32]

Clearly, this touches on two other key concepts of ideological struggle: power and ownership. Power in the liberal capitalist system is exercised to a considerable extent through property. The ideological dimension is vividly illustrated in the suggestion of what amounts to a kind of treason levelled by a distinguished member of the governing Labour Party in Britain against – of all people – the former wartime prime minister, Winston Churchill:

> What is it that enables the right hon. Gentleman [Churchill] to embrace with joyous abandon this supra-national authority outlined in the Schuman declaration and yet to reject the nationalisation of industries at home? The answer is that the common factor which runs through all the actions and speeches of the right hon. Gentleman in his long career is the ruthless determination to defend at all costs the privileges of the class to which he belongs . . . The truth is that the right hon. Gentleman is now prepared to yield power and responsibility if only ownership remains intact. He is prepared to go outside this country to seek a muzzle for Socialism at home.[33]

Churchill was accused – in exaggerated language of a kind to which British MPs sometimes resort during heated, 'Punch-and-Judy'-type debates in the House of Commons – of disloyalty to his country for supporting proposals for cooperation with France and Germany in the cause of European integration. What matters more in this quotation is the question of ownership. That is the commitment either to private ownership on the Conservative side, or to nationalized ownership of the commanding heights of the economy, as implemented by the Labour government under Clement Attlee. For Hayek, this transfer of ownership has the most serious consequences.

> This remains true even though many liberal socialists are guided in their endeavours by the tragic illusion that by depriving private individuals of the power they possess in an individualist system, and by transferring this power to society, they can thereby extinguish power. What all those who argue in this manner overlooked is that by concentrating power so that it can be used in the service of a single plan, it is not merely transferred but infinitely heightened; that by uniting in the hands of some single body power formerly exercised independently by many, an amount of power is created infinitely greater than any that existed before.[34]

Such a concentration of power was of course dangerous in Hayek's eyes, and so were those exercising it, because eventually planning must establish a hierarchy, a command structure of military stamp.[35] From Hayek's point of view, such hierarchies leave no room for entrepreneurship, which is the lifeblood of innovation and therefore social progress.[36] On the contrary, the economy will run along military lines of order, which will lead to a Spartan society, including directed and forced labour such as that Hayek saw in the Arbeitsdienst in Nazi Germany.[37]

In addition, it would propel the most ruthless characters right to the top. 'Since it is the supreme leader who alone determines the ends, his instruments must have no moral convictions of their own.'[38] He is omnipotent and bound by no rules. Below such 'leaders', the system would be saturated by the most corrupt personalities – Hayek cites the Himmlers (head of the SS) and the Heydrichs (head of the SO, the secret service charged with the execution of the annihilation of Jews in the so-called 'final solution')[39] as examples – since favours and status would count more than result.

Such arbitrariness also runs sharply counter to another fundamental tenet of liberalism, the rule of law:

> Indeed, the Rule of Law . . . should probably be regarded as the true opposite of the rule of status. It is the Rule of Law, in the sense of the rule of formal law, the absence of legal privileges of particular people designated by authority, which safeguards that equality before the law which is the opposite of arbitrary government.[40]

Beyond the loss of personal freedom, normally underpinned by the certainty of the law, such arbitrary government must also unsettle the whole logic of the economy in that 'who knows whom' becomes more important than genuine workplace skills. Obviously, this must lead to poorer performance of the economy as a whole, which has to be compensated by further coercive measures of the type the Gestapo was using.

In sum, planning as the core policy of socialism is, from Hayek's perspective, the very point at which the perversion of freedom starts. Hayek agrees here with Adam Smith that government under a doctrine of planning is bound to be oppressive of its subjects and tyrannical by its very nature.[41]

8

Liberty and Totalitarianism

According to Hayek, economic planning leads almost inevitably to totalitarianism, regardless of whether it is called fascism or communism (the prime examples at the time Hayek was writing). He argued that once begun, planning will penetrate all aspects of society, which will need more and more planning in order to remedy the original evil and the consequent failures.[1] Hayek had little patience with the high ideals under the banner of which communist ideals, in particular, were sold, for example: 'greater freedom in the pursuit of higher values ... plain living and high thinking ... reliev[ing] ourselves from the excessive care for material ends.'[2] The most pervasive example of idealistic communist writing was, and arguably still is, Marx and Engels's *Communist Manifesto* of 1848.[3] Hayek is very much in line with Isaiah Berlin, who along with Hayek was one of the most influential liberal thinkers of the twentieth century, in condemning such facile utopianism:

> To threaten a man with prosecution unless he submits to a life in which he exercises no choices of his goals; to block before him every door but one, no matter how noble the prospect upon which it opens, or how benevolent the motives of those who arranged this, is to sin against the truth that he is a man, a being with a life of his own to live.[4]

One might call this the unequivocal rejection of a utopian paradise or the confirmation that choice alone can provide freedom, which thus is the basis of a 'good' life in a liberal world. For Hayek, the link between economic freedom and general liberty is direct:

> Unfortunately, the assurance people derived from this belief that the power which is exercised over economic life is a power over matters of secondary importance only, and which makes them take lightly the threat to the freedom of our economic pursuits, is altogether unwarranted. It is largely a consequence of the erroneous belief that there are purely economic ends separate from the other ends of life ... The ultimate ends of the activities of reasonable beings are never economic. Strictly speaking there is no 'economic motive' but only economic factors conditioning our striving for other ends. What in ordinary language is misleadingly called the 'economic motive' means merely the desire for general opportunity, the desire for power to achieve unspecified ends. If we strive for money it is because it offers us the widest choice in enjoying the fruits of our efforts. Because in modern society it is through the limitation of our money incomes that we are made to feel the restrictions which our relative poverty still imposes upon us.[5]

Hayek refers to the abolition of money because this was a topic, however drastic, enthusiastically discussed during the Great Depression. 'Back to the land' and a return to barter societies were sometimes seriously mooted as solutions to the crisis, but – unsurprisingly – the moneyless society was rejected by both Hayek and Keynes as a fool's paradise, because although money is only a means in economic life, it is a vital one. Keynes was fully in agreement:

> Money in its significant attributes is, above all, a subtle device for linking the present to the future; and we cannot

even begin to discuss the effect of changing expectations on current activities, except in monetary terms. We cannot get rid of money, even by abolishing gold and silver and legal tender instruments. So long as there exists any durable asset, it is capable of possessing monetary attributes and, therefore, of giving rise to the characteristic problems of a monetary economy.[6]

Thus money is not the problem, but, for Hayek, the loss of economic freedom as outlined in Keynesian planning, in socialist policies, and finally in the totalitarian consequences of Nazism and communism, was the beginning of the internal corruption of a people, the thin edge of a truly dangerous wedge. Once unleashed, such corruption can hardly be stopped, Hayek said, because the state will find it necessary to control all aspects of life: 'according to a unitary plan, a "social" view about what ought to be done must guide all decisions. In such a world we should soon find that our moral code is full of gaps.'[7] No such unitary plan can exist, unless it is imposed by the state on the people; therefore, for Hayek, no such unitary plan *should* exist.

Considering human social development, Hayek claimed that rules had steadily become less important, to the point that in modern society genuine individual freedom was achievable. Fewer taboos hindered personal development in liberal societies and formerly rigid constraints of manners and morals had declined in importance to the extent that they had become no more than a broad framework in which everyone could move freely:[8]

the individuals should be allowed, within defined limits, to follow their own values and preferences rather than somebody else's, that within these spheres the individual's system of ends should be supreme and not subject to any dictation by others. It is this recognition of the individual as the ultimate judge of his ends, the belief that as far as possible his own views ought to govern his actions, that forms the essence of the individualist position.[9]

Totalitarian systems cannot handle such personal freedom, because dissent or even novelty cast doubt upon the unitary cause at the centre of totalitarian societies.[10] These come in different shapes and forms and with different prophecies, such as Aryan superiority, infallibility of the proletarian vanguard, victory in the Second World War – again, these were the prime examples in Hayek's time. In opposition to individualism as defined by Hayek, collectivism as used in these totalitarian regimes gives preference to the group over the individual.[11] This was the great nightmare of liberals such as Isaiah Berlin, who made a famous distinction between a positive and a negative concept of liberty. The negative one is fortified by the classical defensive right of non-interference from or by others. Coercion in this sense is the deliberate interference of other human beings, which prevents the individual from enjoying a proper degree of liberty.

> The liberals of the first half of the nineteenth century correctly foresaw that liberty in this 'positive' sense could easily destroy too many of the 'negative' liberties that they held sacred. They pointed out that the sovereignty of the people could easily destroy that of the individual.[12]

Modern liberal societies had been created on the basis of individual freedom and had defined the limits of individualism through such negative liberties, which provide 'freedom from' the interference in the individual's personal affairs.

Totalitarian ideology turned this logic upside down and proclaimed 'freedom to' work, for example. This positive liberty would lead to the dictatorship of the masses. Through positive liberties, totalitarian propaganda would corrupt people and turn citizens into a single-minded mass convinced of one common purpose, in order to maintain unity of a large population such as that of a country. The totalitarian state must make sure that dissidents are rooted out. Outsiders – or those who can plausibly be treated as such – will have to be found for use as scapegoats and as the justification for repression, such as the Jews in Nazi Germany.[13] Coercion to shape even the conscience of the people would be required, notably by propaganda.[14] Isaiah Berlin evokes the Jacobins of the French Revolution and later the communist doctrine that 'Freedom is not freedom to do what is irrational, or stupid, or wrong. To force empirical selves into the right pattern is no tyranny, but liberation.'[15] Hayek described this inversion of right and wrong as corrupted arbitrariness without absolute true values that could act as guidelines of right and wrong:

> Though we may sometimes be forced to choose between different evils, they remain evils. The principle that the end justifies the means is in individualist ethics regarded as the denial of all morals. In collectivist ethics it becomes necessarily the supreme rule; there is literally nothing which the consistent collectivist must not be prepared to do if it serves 'the good of the whole', because the 'good of the whole' is to him the only criterion of what ought to be done . . . There can be no limit to what its citizen must not be prepared to do, no act which his conscience must prevent him from committing, if it is necessary for an end which the community has set itself or which his superiors order him to achieve.[16]

The SS and concentration camps in Nazi Germany and the KGB and Gulags in the USSR were the inherently necessary executive organs of their totalitarian regimes and, for Hayek, the most abhorrent ideological fallacies.[17] Collectivism calls for commonly accepted and enforced rules, goals and a code of conduct from which no one must stray.[18] Naturally, Hayek utterly disapproved:

The essential point for us is that no such complete ethical code exists. The attempt to direct all economic activity according to a single plan would raise innumerable questions to which the answer could be provided only by a moral rule, but to which existing morals have no answer and where there exists no agreed view on what ought to be done ... Not only do we not possess such an all-inclusive scale of values: it would be impossible for any mind to comprehend the infinite variety of different needs of different people which compete for the available resources.[19]

Thus Hayek's rejection of such totalitarian regimes as that introduced by the Nazis in Germany is forceful and uncompromising. Instead, he called for a 'healthy contempt and dislike of power which only an old tradition of personal liberty creates'.[20] This he found in Britain at the time, a remarkable tribute to what he saw as one of the greatest achievements, in respect of the individual as well as in societal terms, of the British.[21]

Hayek further argued that the Nazis had proved that the evil would not stop at the mere internal corruption of a people. Totalitarian systems are bound to expand. They need the spoils of war to be doled out among the supporters. The primary example of the time was the evil which Hayek and his contemporaries saw exploding in Nazi Germany. In this vein, the British ambassador in Berlin from April 1937 to the declaration of war on 3 September 1939, Nevile Henderson, made no bones, on his return, of his view that 'Hitler never intended the ultimate end to be other than war.'[22] This cancer would spread, because it could not stop at internal conquest; neither could it stop at frontiers. It would develop justifications such as Hitler's *Lebensraum* (living space) policy, which claimed that it was only a matter of justice that Germany should wrest territory from its neighbours. For Hayek, this was the most manifest proof of evil: when wrong is dressed up, utterly spuriously, as right.

Hayek's theory of totalitarianism evolved in the post-war period, when much the same charges were levelled against the USSR. Clement Attlee, the British Labour prime minister from 1945 to 1951, fully shared this negative evaluation of the threat of communism in the post-war period:

> Communism is a militant and imperialist creed held with fanaticism by its adherents. It is based on certain ideas. You cannot confute ideas by armed forces. You can confute them by better ideas and by better action and by showing in practice the superiority of the democratic way of life. Military defences against Communism are essential, but they are not a complete policy.[23]

This shows the struggle of ideologies in the Cold War. It also seems to underpin one of Hayek's initial arguments, namely that socialism must inevitably turn into aggressive communism, which would then consume its own founders. Relatively docile leaders such as Lenin had given way to much more aggressive dictators such as Stalin. The relatively mild militants of Versailles had become the merciless *incorruptibles* of the Comité du salut public (Committee of Public Safety). The great military expansion and success of the USSR during the Second World War could still be seen as a defensive reaction to the Nazi attack. The development of nuclear weapons, which the USSR had acquired by 1949, and communist expansionism in the late 1940s and early '50s in Eastern Europe and East Asia were definitely seen as threats in the West.

This was, importantly, not only the evaluation of conservatives in the post-war period, but in fact a Labour prime minister who condemned communism and prepared Britain for another war, should the Soviet Union launch an attack. And in West Germany – the front line in the Cold War in Europe – the fiercest opposition to internal communist subversion and the external communist threat came not so much from the right as from the Social Democrats:

The Communist system means denial of human rights and the enslavement of the working people; it perpetuates hunger, poverty and exploitation. The Communist leaders are the true warmongers against their own people. (strong applause from the SPD to the BP [right-wing Bavaria Party]).[24]

It was former communists, such as Herbert Wehner of the SPD, who had seen the communist system at work in the Soviet Union, and social democrat leaders such as Kurt Schumacher who were most hostile to communism.

By contrast, Hayek tends to see socialism and communism as on a continuum, a spectrum of linked concepts. He does this despite being fully aware of the uncompromising opposition between social democrats and communists during the Weimar Republic and on the left in Britain. In fact, the gap between socialists and communists widened steadily in the post-war period. Of course, some of these developments occurred later than the time when Hayek was writing *The Road to Serfdom*. However, when Hayek seeks, almost wilfully it sometimes seems, to trace a continuum between socialism and communism where there are in fact major differences, he distorts history and reality.

This exposes one of the weaknesses of Hayek's totalitarian theory: as a comprehensive explanation of phenomena, it is always in danger of oversimplifying complex situations. Moreover, although quite discerning analyses have demonstrated considerable affinities relating fascism and communism under totalitarianism, this approach dangerously overlooks important differences.[25] Hayek is again oversimplifying when he disregards the cleavage between communism and socialism, which reaches back to the very roots of left-wing politics.[26] The claim to social leadership of the working class is common to both of them. The way to get there is not. This division was executed notably between Karl Kautsky and Lenin on the issue of the resort to violence. On the one hand, socialists remained loyal to their belief that the superiority of the ideas of the working class would win through in a democratic deliberation process.[27] This is conveyed by the very name Social Democrats. On the other hand, communists sought to bring about the dictatorship of the proletariat, which entailed the use of coercion and violence against those who stood in their way – the ruling middle classes or bourgeoisie. Very much according to Hayek's worst fears, this struggle was believed to be necessary to speed up the course of history and bring about the communist millennium.

In addition to the fundamental difference in political values, the division in economic policy preferences also became more pronounced between communists and socialists in the post-war period. While the communist bloc established command economies, the Social Democrats in Germany – once themselves Marxists, albeit *constitutional* and parliamentary Marxists – abandoned classical paradigms, such as the nationalization of key industries and the command economy. The pragmatic change wrought by the SPD at Bad Godesberg in 1959 marked the beginning of a general trend, and all other socialist parties followed suit in subsequent years, if not in name then certainly in spirit. The French Socialist Party still has nationalization in its manifesto, but since the early, very difficult and instructive years of the presidency of François Mitterrand, such aspirations have decreased in importance to the extent that few now take them seriously. The British Labour Party clung firmly to the principles of public ownership and planning until well into the 1970s – partly, perhaps, because there was no substantial communist party in Britain which could fly this particular banner. By the time Tony Blair came to power in 1997, nationalization and economic planning – following the apparently very successful Thatcherite revolution – were no longer serious policy options for Labour. They had been tried by previous Labour governments and found grievously wanting, singularly unsuited to any solution of the problems of 'declinism' that had beset the British economy since long before the Second World War. In addition, Margaret Thatcher's ferocious assault on the trade unions had left them disheartened, debilitated and, in the eyes of many, discredited.[28]

There can thus be no doubt as to the fundamental difference between communists and socialists in basic attitudes towards political values, such as democracy and economic policy. Hayek ignores this fact, which must cast some doubt upon his development of totalitarian theory, if not for the Nazi period than at least after the Second World War. His blind spot here might also be seen as an indication that ideological tension, such as in the Cold War, can make even the strongest minds – to which group there is no doubt that Hayek belongs – distort evidence to fit a nice ideological theory. Clearly, there were totalitarian elements common to the Nazis and the USSR, but the socialist drive for equality and social justice should not be confused with this. To lose sight of the differences between socialists and communists risks making reality fit ideology, and this has inevitably undermined the forcefulness, even the plausibility, not just of Hayek's theory of totalitarianism, but of his work taken as a whole.

This observation is also valid in respect of his criticism of Keynes, who himself recognizes the advantages of the liberal system:

the modern classical theory has itself called attention to various conditions in which the free play of economic forces may need to be curbed or guided. But there will still remain a wide field of exercise of private initiative and responsibility. Within this field the traditional advantages of individualism will still hold good. Let us stop for a moment to remind ourselves what these advantages are. They are partly advantages of efficiency – the advantages of decentralisation and of the play of self-interest. The advantage to efficiency of the decentralisation of decisions and of individual responsibility is even greater, perhaps, than the nineteenth century supposed; and the reaction against the appeal to self-interest may have gone too far. But above all, individualism, if it can be purged of its defects and its abuses, is the best safeguard of personal liberty in the sense that, compared with any other system, it greatly widens the field for exercise of personal choice. It is also the best safeguard of the variety of life, which emerges precisely from this extended field of personal choice, and the loss of which is the greatest of all the losses of the homogeneous totalitarian state. For this variety preserves the traditions which embody the most secure and successful choices of former generations; it colors the present with the diversification of its fancy; and being the handmaid of experiment as well as of tradition and of fancy, it is the most powerful instrument to better the future.[29]

However, where liberalism falls short, from a Keynesian perspective, is in its failure to understand the problem of unemployment, or rather the view liberalism takes that labour is just another 'good', to be traded in the same way as any other. Classical liberal theory is unambiguous: 'Labour is a commodity like every other, and rises and falls according to demand.'[30] Keynes, whatever he may have thought of the inhuman nature of this statement, argued that it did not make *economic* sense and threatened the political stability of the democracies in the West:

The authoritarian state systems of today seem to solve the problem of unemployment at the expense of efficiency and of freedom. It is certain that the world will not much longer tolerate the unemployment which, apart from brief intervals of excitement, is associated and in my opinion, inevitably associated with present-day capitalistic individualism. But it may be possible by a right analysis of the problem to cure the disease whilst preserving efficiency and freedom.[31]

Against the backdrop of the Great Depression, unemployment was the most important threat to the liberal democracies. Keynes calls for and offers a remedy to the shortcomings of the system, that is, its disregard for employment, or rather policies treating the worker as merely one more good on the market. To have clung obstinately to an ideological system that had manifestly proved fallacious and incapable of handling the Great Depression was, from Keynes's perspective, not remotely in the interest of preserving the merits of the liberal market system as outlined above. He adds that full employment should in fact be the prime objective of economic policy in order to preserve, politically, the liberties in Western democracies. Full employment would, under normal circumstances, increase consumption and not the inverse, as liberals feared, because people would have their wages to spend:

> With normal psychological suppositions, an increase in employment will only be associated with a decline in consumption if there is at the same time a change in the propensity to consume – as the result, for instance, of propaganda in the time of war in favour of restricting individual consumption; and it is only in this event that the increased employment in investment will be associated with an unfavourable repercussion on employment in the industries producing for consumption.[32]

Here Keynes really makes the economic case for the demand side, where liberals feared that such a 'rigging' or manipulation of the market – through the principal interest rate and state investment programmes – would lower efficiency and productivity and undermine the main rationale for individual economic activity, namely, profit. The profit rationale, for Hayek, was the very beginning of economy and freedom.

For his economic model, Keynes assumed relative stability for components such as 'tastes and habits of the consumer, the disutility of different intensi[t]ies of labor and of the activities of supervision and organizations as well as the social structure.'[33] However, it was precisely the radical changes in these structures that marked the 1930s and 1940s and which Hayek described very persuasively. Here Hayek's narrative description in *The Road to Serfdom* of the changes in the aftermath of the Great Depression is much more convincing than an economic theory, which by definition has to be based on certain unchanging foundations, or independent variables, in economic jargon. Such fundamental assumptions are the untold truths behind economic theories and for once Hayek seems to have a more convincing story to tell about why these changes in social structures occur. Keynes stayed with the economic argument that unemployment was the consequence of a malfunctioning liberal market economy, failures inherent in the system, which he proposed to remedy by turning the classical economic rationale on its head. Both men agreed that the merits of the liberal market economy must be preserved, among them, most importantly, the maintenance of freedom.

This commitment to freedom poses, in the final analysis, the question as to whether power is a tool with which to achieve the betterment of men and their environment, or whether it is an end in itself. If it becomes an end in itself, as for Lenin or Stalin, the danger of corruption is great. The point about power is also where the connection to Hayek can ultimately be made. Because of the dangers of the corruption by power which he saw inherent in socialism and communism, he drew the conclusion that it was dangerous to follow this path and that no related ideas, least of all planning, should be entertained. However, is the classical liberal alternative – free-for-all market economy without state planning of any kind – viable? The sole guiding principle of economic activity would be profit – perhaps only immediate profit. Everyone would have the freedom to choose their field of activity, their line of work, their place of work and their family environment. The role of the state would be sharply reduced to that of a sort of political caretaker or night watchman, such as is evoked in the social contract of Rousseau, Hobbes or Locke.[34] It would handle the five classic state activities:

external affairs, protection of the realm, public order (policing), justice and finance – but finance only as needed to fund the other vital services. In every other field, it would leave the citizen entirely to his or her own various devices. This was how classical liberals saw the function of the state; in the words of Burke: 'My opinion is against an over-doing of any sort of administration, and more especially against this most momentous of all meddling on the part of authority; the meddling with the subsistence of the people.'[35]

Moreover, such a state would pose no threat to its neighbours. This is the world according to classical liberal theory, with Hayek as one of its strongest and most plausible advocates.[36] This features, of course, the liberal 'conviction that where effective competition can be created, it is a better way of guiding individual efforts than any other'.[37] No social control is necessary in such a free system and individual choice will prevail in all aspects of life. Competition obviates the need for coercive interference with economic life.[38] Is it really that simple?

9
International Organizations and European Integration

ould we really go back to the minimalist state which does not interfere in private (economic) matters and which could stand alone in 'splendid isolation' from the rest of the world? When writing during the Second World War, Hayek did perceive that, politically, not even Britain was an island. Some freedoms have to be curtailed and domestically some essential services cannot possibly be adequately provided by private individuals, whatever the market incentive.

> Thus neither the provision of signposts on the roads, nor, in most circumstances, that of the roads themselves, can be paid for by every individual user. Nor can certain harmful effects of deforestation, or of some methods of farming, or of the smoke and noise of factories, be confined to the owner of the property in question or to those who are willing to submit to the damage for an agreed compensation. In such instances we must find some substitute for the regulation by the price mechanism.[1]

In addition, the Second World War, during which Hayek was writing, showed inescapably the reality of worldwide relationships and worldwide consequences of quite localized action. In that sense, this war might well be seen as marking the definitive enthronement of a globalization logic from which the world had still held back after the First World War, when – despite the creation of a League of Nations – the major powers, disastrously, withdrew into their spheres of interest: the U.S. immediately, Germany soon after, then France and Britain. The Second World War was the best proof that isolation – 'splendid' or otherwise – could no longer be maintained in a world where ever stronger bonds were being forged between nations, and that not only was isolation no longer possible, but self-interest might actually be a mainspring of world conflict:

> [that] there is little hope of international order or lasting peace so long as every country is free to employ whatever measures it thinks desirable in its own immediate inter-est, however damaging they may be to others, needs little emphasis now.[2]

The reasoning is perfectly simple. Without an international order and international institutions, the only remedy for disputes between states is war. Hayek's liberal forebears had well realized that and had indeed hoped that economic competition could replace war and its consequent suffering. Both wars had led to monstrous economic hardship. This was the ultimate reason for the creation of an international forum such as the League after the First World War. Despite its failure, the victorious Allies set up a successor organization, the United Nations Organisation (UNO), after the Second World War.

Following the internationalization logic, Jean Monnet in his 'Algiers Memorandum' advocated ideas of supra-national economic planning as a solution.[3] Hayek remained sceptical. Internationalization would obviously avoid problems of nationalism and extreme economic selfishness such as that practised under the autarky policy of Nazi Germany, but why should planning work on an international level when it was bound to fail – according to his rationale – at national level?[4] Even worse, imposing the will of a 'supra-national authority'[5] must entail coercion, because there could not be any natural loyalty of the type national institutions commanded and which made court rulings, for example, acceptable and easily enforceable. Anticipating the problem of 'democratic deficit', of which so much has indeed been made in the present-day EU, Hayek argued that the British people would never submit to being outvoted by others in matters which concerned their own country. True as this may have been in 1944, Hayek wildly overreaches himself when he says that such a supranational regime has been successfully implemented only under the Nazi banner of a master race using force.[6] However, a few pages later he expresses this in a format which is less emotionally charged:

> while nations might abide by formal rules on which they have agreed, they will never submit to the direction which international economic planning involves – that while they may agree on the rules of the game, they will never agree on the order of preference in which the rank of their own needs and the rate at which they are allowed to advance is fixed by majority vote . . . they would soon find out that what they have delegated is not merely a technical task, but the most comprehensive power over their very lives.[7]

This kind of reasoning is very relevant in the context of two post-war phenomena. First, the very widespread reticence among British leaders, opinion formers and to no small extent among the ordinary voters in the matter of European integration, that is, supra-nationalism, and, conversely, their robust attachment to national sovereignty. Second, it is true that the European Commission generally has refrained from active interference in the economy, emphasizing much more heavily, with the firm support of the European Court of Justice, the promotion and enforcement of competition over a 'level playing field' on which the same rules apply to each and every competitor in the market, regardless of nationality, within the Union. Again, very much in the vein of British think-ing of the time, Hayek suggested that political integration must precede economic integration if control is to be legitimate. This was sharply in contrast with the ideas of Jean Monnet – the brain behind early European integration ideas – and, in fact, with how European integration actually developed in the post-war period. One can see very clearly the British attachment to national sov-ereignty reflected in British post-war policies of support for the Council of Europe or the Organisation for European Economic Co-operation (OEEC). Importantly, these organizations entirely avoided any serious encroachment on national sovereignty, so that any decision proposed within them could be vetoed by a single country – the classical definition of what is known in political theory as 'intergovernmentalism'.

Organizations such as the OEEC and the Council of Europe were the first attempts to achieve European integration after the war. However, in this respect, at any rate, they led nowhere. Nations blocked each other in the intergovernmental decision-making processes, and only the supranational model of the European Communities – the European Coal and Steel Community (ECSC, 1951), the European Economic Community and Euratom (1958) – showed that faster and generally more beneficial progress was possible under this new and considerably more ambitious approach.

This leads to the question, today, of whether European fed-eration is possible. Under supranationalism, national sovereignty is transferred to institutions above the nation state – such as the European Commission, the European Parliament, the European Court of Justice or, more recently, the European Central Bank (ECB) – empowered to enact legislation binding on the member states. In Britain, this approach is often categorized as 'federation', which had meant, in the British political context, a weak central power which was dependent on the goodwill of its constituent member states. In British history, this was not considered a very attractive scheme, because it was seen as the reason for British weakness in comparison to foreign powers during several historical periods.[8] Considering this and Hayek's previous positions on sovereignty, he, surprisingly, accepted federalism as

> the only form of association of different people which will create an international order without putting an undue strain on their legitimate desire for independence. Federalism is, of course, nothing but the application to international affairs of democracy, the only method of peaceful change man has yet invented. But it is a democracy with definitely limited power.[9]

Monnet would have wholeheartedly agreed. This was the avenue European integration took and although Britain came to be known as the 'awkward partner',[10] it eventually limped into what is now the EU in 1973, though not without many misgivings, which persist to this day – the Brexit vote being the most recent example.

Hayek's greatest achievement may be that he recognized the political concept of federalism as the missing element in the original liberal theories of the nineteenth century.[11] Federalism is a political system that can moderate between nations and thus, he hoped, prevent any recurrence of the atrocities of war, from which Europe was still suffering when Hayek was writing *The Road to Serfdom*. His final words on federation resemble more and more what the EU has turned out to be: 'Neither an omnipotent super-state, nor a loose association of "free nations", but a community of nations of free men must be our goal.'[12] Hayek agrees with Monnet's concept that any international organization should be 'limited in scope, but strong in its executive powers.'[13] That is exactly what happened in specialized communities, such as the ECSC of 1951 – that is, 'sectoral' integration, limited to coal and steel, but with strong powers to harmonize the market in these fields through binding rules and regulations on the member states. Moreover, gradual enlargement from a core group in Western Europe is also what Hayek suggested.[14] This is in fact exactly how the EU has developed in the enlargement process from six founding members in 1951 to 28 member states when Croatia joined in 2013.

After the Second World War, there was widespread agreement that all previous wars had been economic wars: that is to say, wars motivated by an economic profit rationale. Internally, there was often social upheaval, which had found its release and compensation in external conflict. What used to be a traditional socialist explanatory pattern won wide acceptance in France, for example, but also in Germany.[15] The logical consequence was that there was no *national* solution offering peace and prosperity. European economic integration was the only way forward.[16] It was, however, also clear that economics did not tell the whole story. All past wars may have had an economic rationale behind them, but the decision for war came from national *political* authorities. The call for European political integration was a direct consequence and followed the same idea of preventing another war in Europe once and for all.[17] The French – whose vulnerability had been cruelly exposed in 1940 – took the lead in the European integration process, though only on discovering, to their dismay, that Britain was unwilling to assume this role. French leadership found its first major initiative in the Schuman Declaration of 1950 and the resulting ECSC.[18] Harking back to avant-gardist socialist reasoning, Guy Mollet – one of the most successful leaders of the French Fourth Republic (1946–58) – went a step further and argued that economic integration was unlikely to succeed without a European political authority guiding it.[19] Economic structures would not be changed without a supporting political will.[20] This rationale relies on the dominant belief at the time that political integration would have to precede economic integration. Hayek shared this idea that a political accord must be struck first, before economic integration can happen. In reality, in Europe and after the Second World War it happened the other way around. Using economic integration to achieve peace was the ground-breaking idea of the Schuman Declaration, which was drafted by Monnet.[21]

Only in the very lucid statement on federation quoted above does Hayek seem to suggest that this was possible.

Keynes disagreed with this appraisal of international organization. He accepted the important role of the state – most likely because it was the only political reality in existence after the Second World War. The UN had just been founded and was already showing signs of strain, because of the Cold War tensions resulting in blockage of the main organs, such as the Security Council. European integration was at the time little more than a dream. However, in his writings, Keynes refers to the state more in terms of its executive powers, which it should use to stimulate the economy: 'The state will have to exercise a guiding influence on the propensity to consume partly through its scheme of taxation, partly by fixing the rate of interest.'[22] Any other institution that can fulfil that function can replace the state in this logic. If we apply Keynes's rationale to the present time and the European Union, the common internal market is seen to provide a perfectly adequate forum for genuinely free competition among European enterprises. Even in the most sensitive field of taxation, harmonization has happened in the EU. Tax *rates* remain the perquisite of the member states, but interest rates are the responsibility of the ECB for the Eurozone countries, and the national central banks for those countries which have retained their own currencies take the decisions of the ECB into consideration.

It seems therefore that in the EU the instruments available to the authorities to guide the economy are still divided under a Keynesian logic, and this poses problems as regards responsibility for economic planning, accountability and also policy implementation.[23] Keynes clearly agrees, in his *General Theory*, with the criticism now widely shared, especially on the left, that austerity does not work. No new investment because of too much saving leads to a continued slump. Keynes would see the present case of Greece as an example of a situation where the classical liberal economic theory has failed. Keynes would advocate a vigorous stimulus programme rather than austerity. He had diagnosed a similar failure in the Great Depression:

In the United States, for example, by 1929 the rapid capital expansion of the previous five years had led cumulatively to the setting up of sinking funds and depreciation allowances, in respect of plant which did not need replacement, on so huge a scale that an enormous volume of entirely new investments was required merely to absorb these financial provisions; and it became almost hopeless to find still more new investment on a sufficient scale to provide for such new saving as a wealthy community in full employment would be disposed to set aside. This factor alone was probably sufficient to cause a slump. And furthermore, since 'financial prudence' of this kind continued to be exercised through the slump by those great corporations which were still in a position to afford it, it offered a serious obstacle to early recovery.[24]

Over-saving and over-cautious investment were thus seen by Keynes as more of a hindrance than a help to (prompt) economic recovery, although he clearly understood the reasons for such institutional and individual behaviour as he witnessed after the Great Depression, and such as we have seen recently after the financial crisis of 2008–9. Even worse, private sector consumption will be sharply discouraged if a crisis leads to a more general change in purchasing behaviour – in what Keynes called 'the propensity to consume'. Individuals and businesses may, by saving more, starve the real economy in need of their money for investment and consumption.

The obstacle to a clear understanding is, in these examples, much the same as in many academic discussions of capital, namely, an adequate appreciation of the fact that capital is not a self-subsistent entity existing apart from consumption. On the contrary, every weakening in the propensity to consume regarded as a permanent habit must weaken the demand for capital as well as the demand for consumption.[25]

However, what an economy in crisis needs is more consumption in the form of purchases on its domestic market. This was really the key definition of the Keynesian desired economic equilibrium: full employment from a corresponding industrial output set by the state, which would nourish the nation – no more and no less:

> But if nations can learn to provide themselves with full employment by their domestic policy (and, we must add, if they can also attain equilibrium in the trend of their population), there need be no important economic forces calculated to set the interest of one country against that of its neighbour.[26]

Was this wishful thinking? With the benefit of hindsight, it is clear that hardly ever has a nation achieved such stability of its employment and its population, not even in Britain in the immediate post-war years, where there was full employment, and not even in post-war Germany during the time of the economic 'miracle'.

The reason might simply be that affluence, which is another word for full employment, attracts those who are relatively poor. Economic immigration has therefore been a reality in all Western liberal economies. And migration has certainly been a fact of life in the EU since its inception. However, the question can be asked at this point whether the nation states were not simply too small for the economic challenges of the twentieth and the twenty-first centuries. This is often seen as one of the reasons for the foundation of the European Union.[27] Setting the economic framework of output determining full employment, as Keynes claims is necessary, could well be the role of the EU. The European Central Bank in the Eurozone already sets interest rates. The independence of the central banks outside the Eurozone could be seen as a moderating factor, which could be one of the reasons why the EU as a whole, if not in all its parts, weathered the financial crisis of 2008–9 relatively well. Under the current EU social and structural funds, there are already investment programmes for those regions, which fall under the threshold of 75 per cent average per capita income in the EU. In this context a larger EU budget – which has been regularly agreed at around 1 per cent of EU gross national income – should be discussed seriously. In order to arrive at a realistic capability for counter-cyclical investment, the EU should be empowered to incur debt – which is currently prohibited under the Treaty (Article 310, para. 1, TFEU). This would mean that borrowed EU funds could be used counter-cyclically to the budgets of its member states; for example, when in certain states there is low investment, such as during the recent financial crisis, the EU could react with high investment from its budget. This could also work as an equalizing factor between different economic situations in member states, such as currently between southern European and northern European countries. The EU, which possesses a quite sophisticated bureaucratic and judicial apparatus, might be seen as a more advanced example of an institution that can interfere with checks in the market for its own good. Its remit goes beyond the nation states; its supranational procedures enable it to limit national power, notably through rulings handed down by the European Court of Justice. And it was set up with an international scope that should allow it to cope better with challenges resulting from globalization. Notably in economic affairs, the EU speaks with one voice on the international stage, such as in the World Trade Organization (WTO), which many believe is a forum within which discussion of challenges to global trade and resulting economic stability can be fruitful.

Against this background of a sophisticated institutional framework based on trust established over many decades, there is a clear argument that the EU offers a better framework than the nation state for the implementation of Keynesian economic policies. The free market principle has been at the heart of the common internal market since its creation and has, however unevenly, produced the kind of affluence liberal economists see rightly as the main economic merit of the market. A Keynesian economic policy framework on the

EU level may have the potential to produce what Keynes promised: full employment and economic equilibrium.

Hayek and Keynes agreed that individuals need in their own lives a measure of planning, which makes it possible for them to make provision for the future. Planning for the individual therefore depends on a relatively stable economic framework. Keynes would find this in the reliable planning of the economic environment, for example in the interest rate; Hayek would argue that the market is the yardstick against which individuals orientate their expectations. As he outlined in his article 'The Use of Knowledge in Society', the sum of these expectations makes up the economy, and the market is the mechanism and the reference point that make it work for all. Hayek summarized this phenomenon as the 'social mind'.[28] It accounts for the coordination of individual action for the common good. The market will distribute scarce resources as if according to a single plan, but, importantly, without conscious control. That phenomenon of the market avoids deliberate abuse, as happened in command economies, but it also relieves political decision takers of this enormous responsibility – which, if they exercised it, must also almost inevitably be unjust. Hayek and Keynes both agree on that merit of the market, although to different degrees, and in Keynes's case clearly with the caveat of the obligation of the elected democratic leaders to set the economic framework for the good of their citizens, but without touching the inner workings of the market. This means that either the state, for Keynes, or the market, for Hayek, must reduce uncertainty in the economy as much as possible, in order to enable individuals to get on relatively smoothly with their own lives. Sharp changes in the economy have always triggered anxiety and unrest, as life's outlook becomes clouded and families feel ever less confident in the plans they must necessarily make for their future. Keynes would argue that the state has to achieve full employment to avoid such uncertainty among the people. Hayek would see the free working of the market, in which the people can seize their opportunities, as the founding principle to guarantee stability.

Keynes referred in this context again to interest rates: 'If the current rate of interest is positive for debts of every maturity, it must always be more advantageous to purchase a debt than to hold cash as a store of wealth. If on the contrary, the future rate of interest is uncertain,'[29] yields from the capital cannot be predicted. He would add that it is the responsibility of the state to provide for predictability in the interest rate. This is clearly a function the market cannot fulfil, at least not as reliably as can a government. However, Keynes also predicted that the tool of low and stable interest rates has its limits. Low interest rates will tend to induce entrepreneurs to invest more, and thus stimulate the economy: 'money is the drink which stimulates the system to activity.'[30] But there is also a point of saturation, which, for Keynes, will be reached at full employment:

> Furthermore, if our assumption is correct that the marginal propensity to consume falls off steadily as we approach full employment, it follows that it will become more and more troublesome to secure a further given increase in employment by further increasing investment.[31]

In reality, we find today that most central banks in developed economies try to avoid substantial or abrupt changes of interest rates. The policy of the ECB also keeps interest rates relatively stable. This is consistent with Keynes's call for a *predictable* financial and monetary policy.

Eventually this leads us back to the question of whether labour is a commodity, as in liberalism, or whether it is seen as a means to provide an income for citizens, so that social peace and, through that, economic equilibrium too will be achieved. Against this background it may be worthwhile to look in more detail at the interest rate, which Keynes suggested as being one major tool for achieving full employment. He stated in *The General Theory* the following about the interest rate:

The influence of changes in the rate of interest on the amount actually saved is of paramount importance, but in the *opposite direction* to that usually supposed ... a rise in the rate of interest will have the effect of reducing the amount actually saved ... [it] will diminish investment; hence a rise in the rate of interest must have the effect of reducing incomes ... when the rate of interest rises, the rate of consumption will decrease. But this does not mean that there will be a wider margin of saving. On the contrary, saving and spending will *both* decrease.[32]

This policy seems to correspond to the current policy of the ECB as well, that is, to keep interest rates low. One might argue that the purpose of this is to stimulate the economy in the Eurozone after the financial crisis. However, in the maintaining of interest rates at a low level in the Eurozone, there is also an element of acceptance of the Keynesian rationale that investment and savings will increase through low interest rates. In contrast, keeping the cost of borrowing low goes against one classical liberal position in favour of encouraging saving through high interest rates. Although it might be argued that high interest rates are more of a conservative fiscal policy than a liberal credo – Keynes referred to the conservative interest rate policy in the United States in the aftermath of the Great Depression[33] – Keynes considered this logic simply wrong:

The rise in the rate of interest might induce us to save more, *if* our incomes were unchanged. But if the higher rate of interest retards investment, our incomes will not, and cannot be unchanged. They must necessarily fall, until the declining capacity to save has sufficiently offset the stimulus to save given the higher rate of interest.[34]

Keynes argued convincingly that classical economic theory is mistaken in using the interest rate to encourage saving. The interest rate, he believed, should be used rather to stimulate the economy for achieving full employment, and that means a generally low interest rate: 'If the rate of interest were so governed as to maintain continuous full employment, Virtue would resume her sway.'[35] He goes on to say that 'for every rate of interest there is a level of employment for which that rate is the "natural" rate, in the sense that the system will be in equilibrium with that rate of interest and that level of employment.'[36]

However, low interest rates alone do not guarantee low un- employment, as we can see today in Spain, Greece and Italy. And one can find in history a variety of rates of interest corresponding to full employment, from which we can infer that other factors are also at play. This means that the interest rate corresponding to any given level of employment depends on the time and space in which it occurred: when, and in what societal context. Keynes thus qualifies:

> I am no longer of the opinion that the concept of a 'natural' rate of interest, which previously seemed to me a most promising idea, has anything useful or significant to con- tribute to our analysis. It is merely the rate of interest which will preserve the *status quo*; and in general, we have no predominant interest in the *status quo* as such. If there is any such rate of interest which is unique and significant, it must be the rate which we might term the *neutral* rate of interest, namely, the natural rate in the above sense which is consistent with *full* employment, given the other parameters of the system; though this rate might be better described, perhaps, as the *optimum* rate.[37]

Here we can see another phenomenon in economic theory, which is recurrent in any social science but which is hardly ever openly men- tioned, namely the acceptance of the importance of change. As we said above, all is dependent on time and space and thus relative to a given environment. Keynes seemed to be more straightforward in conceding this need for relativity in economic theory, and he argued for making that inevitable change as predictable as possible. Social sciences and particularly economics are obsessed with the definition of independent and dependent variables. The definition depends, however, always on the context, and thus any choice is arbitrary – although it is hoped to be the right choice at a given point in time and space.

It is important to realize that change is omnipresent and important for the progress of our society. For an economic analysis this means that independent variables can become dependent ones, and that this depends not only on the choice of a specific study, but on fundamental changes in our societies.[38] What remains as the essential message of *The General Theory* is that 'the volume of output depends solely on the assumed constant level of employment in conjunction with the current equipment and techniques; and we are safely ensconced in a Ricardian world.'[39] This means that from the interest rate follows a level of industrial output and corresponding employment. Keynes advocated use of the interest rate for the social good of achieving full employment, rather than leaving it free-floating or artificially high, as in laissez-faire liberal economic dispositions of the 1930s. Clearly, the Keynesian view that the interest rate should be used as a tool with which to achieve full employment seems to correspond more to a general desire for control over the economy than the liberal premise that the market should be left to its own devices, where labour would be a commodity pretty well like any other, and the interest rate would be at best a lure to foreign investors.

However, it has been pointed out that one fundamental problem with Keynesian economics is entrepreneurial anticipation of the market. Businessmen and speculators, with a little foresight, can use state intervention in the market, such as a change of the interest rate, for their particular advantage and motivation: common profit-seeking. This means that not only would the intervention of the state itself cause market distortion; so to would the corresponding actions of traders in the market. Classical liberal theory described the problem as follows:

The moment that Government appears at market, all principles of market will be subverted. I don't know whether the farmer [representing the entrepreneur] will suffer by it, as long as there is a tolerable market of competition; but I am sure that, in the first place, the trading government will speedily become bankrupt, and the consumer in the end will suffer.[40]

George Soros, one of the most prominent speculators, calls this 'double distortion' of the free market, first by government and then by the anticipating trader, a 'reflexive feedback loop'.[41] An example can be seen when he took heavy positions against the pound sterling leading to the breakdown of the (European) Exchange Rate Mechanism, under which arrangement the Bank of England had undertaken to hold fluctuations of the currency within a range of +/−2.25 per cent against a given reference – which was at this time the European Currency Unit (ECU). This commitment by the Bank of England proved impossible to respect, not least because of the heavy speculation against it.[42] The liberal counter-argument against such economic frameworks is thus that they can become a cause of the economic problems themselves. The example often cited in this context is the comparison of French with West German economic policy throughout the post-war period. West Germany – CDU/CSU and SPD governments alike – generally signed up to a freer social market economy, guaranteeing monetary stability through the Bundesbank (Federal Bank). France pursued an active economic policy of state intervention for the sake of the social good (*l'état tutélaire*), notably, of course, to combat unemployment. Economies 'rigged', or at any rate manipulated, in that way were essentially found to be less competitive than economies run under free market economy principles, such as Germany's.[43] This is seen as one of the reasons for the relatively faster growth of German economic strength in comparison with that of France, and it is a good example, casting the effectiveness of Keynesian economics into doubt.

Conclusion

The logic outlined at the end of the previous chapter leads to the question, how then can economic sustainability be achieved? We have seen that both Keynesianism and liberalism are fraught with problems of logic and plausibility, but that both Keynes and Hayek have original arguments that have proved hard to refute. Beyond the theoretical discussion, the question arises as to where planning and freedom are, or should be, located: at the individual level or at the level of the state. Choice, as the big postulate of Enlightenment and, for that matter, of liberalism, is normally individual choice.[1] The choice of governments must be to decide how much regulation will be necessary to prevent financial crises – the EU had been suggested as a suitable level for such regulation to operate on. However, it is also the choice of each individual as to how much profit one wishes to make with one's money. Unrestrained greed seems to have been one of the basic factors leading to the latest financial crisis. The 'get rich quick' culture has also produced, or at any rate greatly widened, a disconnection between the real economy and the highly speculative stock market. Keynes had this to say:

> I see, therefore, the rentier aspect of capitalism as a transitional phase which will disappear when it has done its work. And with the disappearance of its rentier aspect much else in it besides will suffer a sea-change. It will be,

moreover, a great advantage of the order of events which I am advocating, that the euthanasia of the rentier, of the functionless investor, will be nothing sudden, merely a gradual but prolonged continuance of what we have seen recently in Britain, and will need no revolution.[2]

A boundless desire for greater and greater wealth has been shown as one of the less savoury elements of liberalism, an element that may still have been acceptable in the eighteenth century – Adam Smith strongly defended it, of course. By the end of the Second World War it had become less acceptable – one of the reasons for which was precisely a financial crisis, leading to the Great Depression. Today, a crisis of these dimensions could bring down the real economy of the whole world. Such a risk is clearly unacceptable. Some moderation of the most libertarian tenets of liberalism – today, what is meant is a degree of 're-regulation' of the financial sector – seems to be in order. The difference may be between making a living by making a profit in the free market, and making a fortune: the spirit of the latter seems to be growth for its own sake. The market incentive, however, privileges exactly that unlimited growth, which leads to the positive effects of progress and increased productivity, as classical liberals such as Adam Smith would claim. However, unlimited progress must at some point also become unsustainable in a closed economic system: an increase in productivity will lead to higher production and therefore (on a transparent market) lower prices, necessitating a constant growth of production just, as it were, to stay even.

The solution usually sought in such circumstances is expansion outside the national economic system, for example in exports. Alternatively, the route of state intervention as regards the volume of production, in the form of price guarantees, can be taken – a spectacular example being the highly controversial earlier stages of the EEC Common Agricultural Policy, under which milk 'lakes' and butter 'mountains' became alarming examples of consequences that were utterly unintended, until ways were found of curbing excess output. The liberal market solution of expansion beyond national markets, for example, seems to be more promising and does not do any harm, at least to the exporter. But what happens if the reference system is no longer the national economy, nor even a regional economy, such as the EU internal market? What happens if one day there is a truly integrated world economy? At this stage of development, the liberal market logic must break down, because there no further expansion is possible outside the system (unless one wanted to consider human migration to other planets, which is as yet not feasible).[3] What we are currently witnessing, however, is on the one hand a change of entrepreneurial activity in the development of new business models, such as non-profit organizations and social businesses.[4] On the other hand, we see a debate around sustainability, which privileges intervention in the market, mainly because within this discourse the world is seen as a closed system, in which the market logic must eventually reach its limits.[5]

It may be worthwhile recalling the still widely accepted definition of sustainable development from the 'Brundtland' report (*Our Common Future*) of 1987. The objective set in the report was to establish patterns of development which would be sustainable for all and result in better life quality for current and future generations through social, economic and environmentally sustainable development.[6] Socially sustainable development, for Keynes, would clearly avoid unemployment, while economically sustainable development would avoid raptor capitalism; and environmentally sustainable development would avoid the depletion of resources and further pollution of the earth. This is, in effect, the description of a more just society, a world in equilibrium: an objective Keynes would agree with. One way to achieve this could be the re-establishment of the link between citizens and the land. Land and habitats are not just investments or consumer goods for citizens, at least not if it is their land. Through their self-interest in the land, real estate owners must be seen as a productive, but also a conserving force in society. Historical examples will always remain wanting, because of differences in societal context, but in Edmund Burke's *Thought and Details on Scarcity*, a good description is nevertheless given of 'the traditional skill and experience of that class of men, who, from father to son, have for generations laboured in calling forth the fertility of the English soil'.[7]

Interestingly, Keynes thought that land could play the same role as money in society, and it had once done so in feudal societies, where loyal services were rewarded with titles (as is still the case in Britain), as well as with land. Thus land can equate to money in its function in society.[8] It cannot be transported as money can – which is the reason for the success of the latter – but the payment function was and can be the same. Ownership of land led to the owners taking diligent care of their property, which seems to provide a combination of profit and sustainability. Market logic would clearly support that argument, as would historical experience. What would have to be achieved under this logic is an extension of ownership which would be supported by a liberal logic, but which would also necessitate full employment in order to enable more people to afford property. This can be seen as a sustainable social, economic and environmental policy.[9] The first two elements are self-evident. Environmentally sustainable development would be achieved through an increased individual interest in the maintenance of land and property, providing for a long-term survival interest through land and property structure. Through the use of land as a means of payment, individual initiative could be harnessed for sustainable development, combining the social and economic welfare of the people with the most important truth of liberal market theory: profit. Hayek and Keynes would probably both agree to this. They come together in the notion that we can and must take action, take responsibility and, by however small a margin, make of our world a better – or, at the very least, a less grossly unfair – place.

Hayek's conclusion, writing in 1943, is pessimistic, even depressing, however:

As is true with respect to other great evils, the measures by which war might be made altogether impossible for the future may well be worse than even war itself. If we can reduce the risk of friction likely to lead to war, this is probably all we can reasonably hope to achieve.[10]

This kind of scepticism, unsurprising in the shadow of the Second World War, serves now to highlight remarkably well what progress has been made. If the only achievement of the EU were that of peace for 65 years, that alone would be a unique step forward in the progress of mankind, the result of a colossal historic synergy wrought by men of remarkable vision. If we add together the remarkable advances in economic integration, which Hayek believed to be nigh on impossible, and the unprecedented material benefits trade expansion has yielded, then we can see his final call for progress as presciently foreshadowing the powerful framework which the EU has now become:

it is more important to clear away the obstacles with which human folly has encumbered our path and to release the creative energy of individuality than to devise further machinery for 'guiding' and 'directing' them – to create conditions favourable to progress rather than to 'plan progress'.[11]

Individual ambition, for Hayek, is the driving force behind our free market economies. For him, this is a force for good. Keynesian 'guiding' and 'directing', he believed, would suppress that ambition and destroy individualism. This was a statement Hayek made against the background of the only economic reality he knew at the time, namely, national economies in competition in the world market. He hinted at a potential evolution of this state of affairs in his chapter on international organizations, but the possibility of an integrated market of several national economies was clearly not foreseeable at the end of the Second World War, certainly not on the scale now reached in the EU.

The EU is also a remarkable illustration of the extent to which reality can exceed by far in complexity even quite sophisticated academic interpretations. Politics in the real world, ever changing, is flexible and seeks to solve concrete problems. It is very different from the opposing juxtapositions of central planning, on the one hand, and market-based competition on the other, which Hayek and Keynes analysed in such detail.[12] In the EU, the two are combined, as in the Common Internal Market, which has untrammelled but 'workable' competition as its basis, but at the same time operates regional, social and structural funds, a central budget and the ECB, which allow a minimum of central steering of the economic development of the Community. These latter instruments in particular could be seen as setting the economic framework called for by Keynes in his *General Theory*. These schemes were put in place in the EU to help create a 'level playing field' of economic competition, which would allow the economically weaker parts of the EU to participate effectively in the economic activities of the common internal market. The EU therefore recognizes that not all entrepreneurs can develop their economic ambitions equally easily, and thus they cannot participate automatically and fully in the internal market on equal terms. These terms have to be created through the economic framework. This philosophy seems to tie in closely with what Keynes had been advocating. He would argue that measures such as those that make the common market equally accessible to every entrepreneur do not destroy individual ambition – which he accepted as the driving force behind economic activity. Rather, these measures can facilitate the fulfilment of economic aspirations for many for whom such success would be otherwise impossible.

One important feature that Hayek identifies in his defence of liberalism is its ruthlessness, which he calls 'the impersonal character of the process'.[13] It has much in common with Adam Smith's almost omnipotent arbitrariness of the invisible hand, which guides economic activities for the greater benefit of all:

it is impossible to foretell who will be the lucky ones or whom disaster will strike, that rewards and penalties are not shared out according to somebody's views about the merits or demerits of different people, but depend on their capacity and their luck ... we should not be able to predict which particular person will gain and which will lose.[14]

This comes perilously close to a fatalistic submission of human fortunes to lightning strikes generated by wanton gods. Applied to our times, some big corporations have used society itself as their lightning rod: witness most notably their behaviour during the financial crisis of 2008–9. Companies that had already paid out handsome dividends to their shareholders then had to be bailed out with public money, which amounts to the internalization of profit and the externalization of risk, as Hayek describes. And here one of the fundamental weaknesses of economic liberalism cannot be concealed: namely, that by its very nature it tends to favour the big and strong economic agents. Once they have become so big that their collapse would endanger the whole economy – 'too big to fail' – they have, because they cannot be allowed to go under, in effect actually achieved full protection from the bolts of lightning that can wipe out smaller enterprises. In terms of the key dichotomy between competition and planning, such effects go far to invalidate Hayek's assertion of the superiority of free competition, because such paradoxical outcomes are neither competitive nor free, but purely and simply a modern form of legalized profiteering. In effect, the freedom won is the freedom of the strong to crush the weak. Here we come back to the original liberal claim that human planning cannot positively influence the economy. But Smith's invisible hand or Hayek's 'impersonal and anonymous mechanism' of the market are concepts the full and extreme implications of which must be unacceptable to any society with a claim to civility. Ordinary human decency will always have problems accepting the gross injustice of personal suffering resulting from the financial crisis, on the one hand, and huge, entirely unearned, windfall profits on the other.

This feeling of injustice accounts for much of the motivation of those who argue that Keynesian economics must be given another try. Hence we may well see the introduction of some Keynesian elements as regards foresight, planning and responsibility, for example in the EU, which already in some areas favours redistributive solutions and the development of an economic framework ensuring equal access to markets. There we find the spirit of justice, of 'fair play', which may well lead in the future to a strengthening of the redistributive policies of the EU.

Economic Theory = Theory of an Ideal Society

One limit to Keynes's *General Theory*, which he imposed himself, is that it is essentially an analysis of the economic system, with relatively little consideration of the consequences for the political system. Most of them remain implicit and are expressed not as political demands, but as economic reasons. This happened deliberately, because Keynes saw himself as an economist and therefore confined himself to the analysis of the economy in order to give his *General Theory* the credibility of thorough, often mathematical, economic analysis, in contrast with other more general, but arguably also more polemical, works, such as Hayek's *Road to Serfdom*. However, this restricted approach became a major shortcoming at the time Keynes was writing. Despite the fact that he made a few political comments in the conclusions to the *General Theory*, they amount really only to a rudimentary analysis of the impact of human nature on the economy:

> Though in the ideal commonwealth men may have been
> taught or inspired or bred to take no interest in the stakes,
> it may still be wise and prudent statesmanship to allow
> the game to be played, subject to rules and limitations, so

long as the average man, or even a significant section of the community, is in fact strongly addicted to the money-making passion.[15]

Human greed as a negative contributing factor to economic instability, for example in the Great Depression, became a major argument, particularly in socialist circles, after the Second World War. It is not the greed of the few, it was argued, but the needs of the many that should be the rationale informing economic decisions.[16] Moreover, the rationale of economic wars became a major influence in left-wing circles during the same period. Keynes put it this way:

War has several causes. Dictators and others such, to whom war offers, in expectation at least, a pleasurable excitement, find it easy to work on the natural bellicosity of their peoples. But over and above this, facilitating their task of fanning the popular flame, are the economic causes of war, namely, the pressure of population and the competitive struggle of markets.[17]

What is interesting as regards the post-war period is that this Keynesian logic, which had long been accepted in socialist circles, became widely accepted even by conservative parties, which would usually subscribe to more liberal economics. This quotation from a conservative German Christian Democrat in the first German Bundestag after the war may serve as an example: 'the wars of recent times have essentially been wars of economic domination. This thought inevitably leads us to trying to bring to an end the competition between national economies.'[18] Both in France and in Germany, the logic of economic wars – wars driven by an economic profit rationale – became widely accepted.[19] Aggressive trade policies (and during the Depression, restrictions to trade), particularly 'beggar-thy-neighbour' policies using prohibitive import tariffs, were also seen as decisions that would help to favour or incite recourse to violence. Keynes agreed with that logic:

the express object [of a state] of upsetting the equilibrium of payments [was] to develop a balance of trade in its own favor. International trade would cease to be what it [had at the time become], namely, a desperate expedient to maintain employment at home by forcing sales on foreign markets and restricting purchases, which, if successful, will merely shift the problem of unemployment to the neighbor . . . but a willing and unimpeded exchange of goods and services in conditions of mutual advantage.[20]

In arguing for free trade and no deficit in the trade balance, Keynes and Hayek would certainly concur.

In his concluding paragraphs, Keynes argues for the power of ideas and particularly economic ideas in that context:

the ideas of economists and political philosophers, both when they are right and when they are wrong, are more powerful than is commonly understood. Indeed the world is ruled by little else. Practical men, who believe themselves to be quite exempt from any intellectual influence, are usually the slaves of some defunct economist. Madmen in authority, who hear voices in the air, are distilling their frenzy from some academic scribbler of a few years back. I am sure that the power of vested interests is vastly exaggerated compared with the gradual encroachment of ideas. Not, indeed, immediately, but after a certain interval; for in the field of economic and political philosophy there are not many who are influenced by new theories . . . ideas which civil servants and politicians and even agitators apply to current events are not likely to be the newest. But, soon or late, it is ideas, not vested interests, which are dangerous for good or evil.[21]

In the Keynesian case, this led to the early application of the principles (later spelled out in *The General Theory*) in the New Deal policy of

President Roosevelt in the United States. And this is where Keynes's economic theory was then put into action and thus became a 'theory of society', just as controversial as liberalism has always been.

From the very outset, Hayek's version of liberalism lent itself more to political considerations. The concept of freedom reveals liberalism as not just an economic theory, but really, primarily, as a theory of the good society and how it should work. In contrast, recent economics have introduced more and more abstraction, and Hayek was one of the driving forces behind this tendency:

> I am certain there are many who regard with impatience and distrust the whole tendency, which is inherent in all modern equilibrium analysis, to turn economics into a branch of pure logic, a set of self-evident propositions which, like mathematics or geometry, are subject to no other test but internal consistency. But it seems that if only this process is carried far enough it carries its own remedy with it. In distilling from our reasoning about the facts of economic life those parts which are truly *a priori* . . . My criticism of the recent tendencies to make economic theory more and more formal is not that they have gone too far, but that they have not yet been carried far enough to complete the isolation of this branch of logic . . . using formal economic theory as a tool in the same way as mathematics.[22]

At the same time, Hayek called for more comprehensive knowledge of how society works and particularly how information is transmitted between different individuals in society: 'pure analysis seems to have so extraordinarily little to say about institutions, such as the press, the purpose of which is to communicate knowledge.'[23] This seems to suggest that the more communication happens, the better it is for the equilibrium of society as a whole, and this would also then provide a more stable economic equilibrium, if economic decisions were based on more reliable data, much greater transparency, and not only of the markets. Clearly, since the time when Hayek and Keynes wrote, the sources of information that are available to individuals have immeasurably increased. The Internet, with its almost unlimited communication capacities, is one of the best examples. The question today is more about which source of information to choose, about the reliability of information and eventually how much information a person can usefully absorb. The available mass of information seems to suggest that everything is or can be known. However, the question of the relevance of information is still the most important, and 'information overflow' does not make decisions about this any easier. This lack of structure, or, rather, the need for it, suggests that economic theory will still have a role to play. Theory, somewhat like ideology, has always had the function of simplifying reality, which has always been complex. Theory tells the reader where to look for information among the amorphous mass and how to structure it to arrive at a coherent understanding of reality. Hayek demanded that theory become an objective analysis of the real world through empirical examination, which would then be the basis on which an economic theory can rest.

Recent economics have followed this call for economic modelling and always increasing mathematics in the discipline. In contrast to Hayek's demand, this does not lead to an empirical understanding of the world. The tendency to turn economics into a quasi-natural science has made it more sterile and removed the main merits of economics from the understanding of all but the most specialized experts in the field. Economics today has become more and more an instrument of – sometimes little more than an exercise in – logic. Keynes saw that danger early on, despite the fact that he was no stranger to mathematical formulae. Economists have tried to push the explanatory potential of the discipline to its limit by making it more and more abstract, 'at the price of leaving more and more obscure what sort of relevance their arguments had to the phenomena of the real world'.[24] Therefore he calls finally also for a return to the 'common-sense meaning of our analysis'.[25] Fundamentally, economic theory has a role to play in the understanding of society and in providing explanations of how society works and how it should work. Ultimately, economists may well have to resort more to narrative and rather less to symbol if their work is to become accessible to a wider global audience.

Abbreviations

CDU	Christlich-Demokratische Union
CSU	Christlich-Soziale Union
JO	*Journal officiel de la République française*
MRP	Mouvement Républicain Populaire
PS	Parti Socialiste
RRS	Républicain radical et radical socialiste
SPD	Sozialdemokratische Partei Deutschlands
UDSR	Union démocratique et socialiste de la Résistance
VDB	Verhandlungen des Deutschen Bundestages
WP	Legislative period of four years (*Wahlperiode* in German)

References

Introduction

1 J. M. Keynes, *The General Theory of Employment, Interest and Money* [1936] (London, 2008).

2 F. A. Hayek, *The Road to Serfdom* (London, 1944), pp. viii, 2.

3 See E. Burke, *Thoughts and Details on Scarcity* (1800, also as a memorandum to PM William Pitt in 1795), para. 4.4.47.

4 A. Smith, *Wealth of Nations* (Oxford, 1993), p. 432.

5 K. Marx, *Das Kapital: Kritik der politischen Ökonomie* [1872] (Cologne, 2000), pp. 377–83, see also Keynes, *General Theory*, p. 244.

6 A. Smith, *The Wealth of Nations* (Glasgow, 1776), see also the work of Milton Friedman, for example.

7 Keynes, *General Theory*, p. 10.

8 F. A. Hayek, 'Economics and Knowledge', *Economica*, vol IV/6 (1937), available at www.econlib.org, accessed 10 July 2015

9 Keynes, *General Theory*, p. 7.

10 Ibid., p. 7.

11 Ibid., p. 9 n. 1 (italics original).

12 Ibid., p. 192.

13 Ibid., p. 197.

14 Hayek, 'Economics and Knowledge', para. 3.5.

15 A. Farrant, 'Knowledge and Incentives: Socialism after Hayek?', *Review of Social Economy*, LXVII/3 (September 2009), p. 383.

1 From the Eighteenth to the Twentieth Century: Momentous Change and Stable Elements

1 J. S. Mill, *Utilitarianism, Liberty and Representative Government* (London, 1910); A. Smith, *The Wealth of Nations* (Glasgow, 1776); D. Hume, *Treatise on Human Nature*; E. Burke, *Sublime and Beautiful* (Milton Park, 2008) and E. Burke, *Thoughts and Details on Scarcity*

(1800), available at Edmund Burke, Miscellaneous Writings, Liberty Fund, www.econlib.org.

2   Burke, *Thoughts and Details on Scarcity*, para. 4.4.6.

3   F. A. Hayek, 'Economics and Knowledge', *Economica* (1937), available at www.econlib.org, para. 3.35.

4   A. Smith, *Wealth of Nations*, see also, Emma Rothschild, 'The Bloody and Invisible Hand', in Emma Rothschild, *Economic Sentiments: Adam Smith, Condorcet and the Enlightenment* (Cambridge, MA, 2001), pp. 116–56.

5   T. Burczak, *Socialism after Hayek* (Ann Arbor, MI, 2006), p. 62.

6   Burke, *Thoughts and Details on Scarcity*, para. 4.4.63 (italics original).

7   A. Farrant, 'Knowledge and Incentives: Socialism after Hayek?', *Review of Social Economy,* LXVII/3 (September 2009), p. 386.

8   F. A. Hayek, *Individualism and Economic Order* (Chicago, IL, 1948), p. 194, quoted ibid. (italics Farrant's).

9   J. M. Keynes, *The General Theory of Employment, Interest and Money* [Cambridge, 1936] (London, 2008), p. 161.

10 F. A. Hayek, *The Road to Serfdom* (London, 1944), Chapter One.

11 Keynes, *General Theory*, p. 8.

12 Burke, *Thoughts and Details on Scarcity*, para. 4.4.38.

13 Hayek, *Road to Serfdom*, p. 19.

14 Burke, *Thoughts and Details on Scarcity,* para. 4.4.18–19, see also 4.4.62; a similar rationale is followed in Burke's opposition to the French Revolution, see E. Burke, *Reflections on the Revolution in France, and Other Writings* (Oxford, 1907).

15 J. M. Keynes, *The Economic Consequences of the Peace* (New York, 1919).

16 Burke, *Thoughts and Details on Scarcity,* para. 4.4.22.

17 Keynes, *General Theory*, p. 154.

18 Ibid.

19 Ibid., p. 155.

20 T. Burczak, 'Hayekian Socialism, Post Critics', *Review of Social Economy*, LXVII/3 (September 2009), p. 391.

2 Hayek's Road to Liberty

1   F. A. Hayek, *The Road to Serfdom* (London, 1944), p. 51.

2   Ibid., p. 52.

3   E. Burke, *Thoughts and Details on Scarcity* [1800], available at Edmund Burke, Miscellaneous Writings, Liberty Fund, www.econlib.org, para. 4.4.38.

4   Hayek, *Road to Serfdom*, p. 52.

5   Ibid.

6   A. Smith, *An Inquiry into the Nature and Causes of the Wealth of Nations* (Oxford, 1976), pp. 455–6.

7   T. Burczak, *Socialism after Hayek* (Ann Arbor, MI, 2006), as quoted in A. Farrant, 'Knowledge and Incentives: Socialism after Hayek?', *Review of Social Economy*, LXVII/3 (September 2009), p. 383.

8   T. Burczak, 'Hayekian Socialism, Post Critics', *Review of Social Economy*, LSVII/3 (September 2009), p. 389; see also J. Runde, 'Information, Knowledge and Agency: The Information Theoretic Approach and Austrians', *Review of Social Economy*, LX/2 (June 2002), p. 184.

9   Burczak, 'Hayekian Socialism, p. 391.

10 J. Runde, 'Information, Knowledge and Agency: The Information Theoretic Approach and the Austrians', *Review of Social Economy*, LX/2 (June 2002), p. 196.

11 Burczak, 'Hayekian Socialism', p. 390.

12 Hayek, *Road to Serfdom*, p. 53.

13 Ibid., p. 55.

14 Ibid.

15 See also Burke, *Thoughts and Details on Scarcity*, para. 4.4.16.

16 T. Burczak, *Socialism after Hayek* (Ann Arbor, MI, 2006), pp. 66–77, as quoted in Farrant, 'Knowledge and Incentives', p. 385, see also p. 386.

17 See T. C. Hörber, *A Converging Post-war European Discourse: War Experience, Changing Security Concepts, and Research and Education* (Lanham, MD, 2014), p. 198.

18 C. de Gaulle, *Mémoires d'espoir* (Paris, 1999), p. 111.

19 Hayek, *Road to Serfdom*, p. 56.

20 Ibid., pp. 57–8.

21 M. Eastman, *The Reader's Digest* (July 1941), p. 39, as quoted in Hayek, *Road to Serfdom*, p. 109.

22 Runde, 'Information, Knowledge and Agency', p. 185.

23 Ibid., p. 193, see also p. 198.

24 Ibid., p. 194; for Austrian views on probability, see K. Popper, *A World of Propensities* (Bristol, 1990). Also see J. Runde, 'On Popper, Probabilities and Propensities', *Review of Social Economy*, 54 (1996), pp. 465–85, and G. P. O'Driscoll. and M. J. Rizzo, *The Economics of Time and Ignorance* (Oxford, 1985).

25 Keynes, *General Theory*, p. 11.

26 Ibid.

27 Ibid., pp. 11–12.

28 Smith, *Wealth of Nations*, see also Keynes, *General Theory*, p. 189.

29 Keynes, *General Theory*, p. 13.

30 Ibid., p. 189.

31 Ibid., p. 171.

32 Ibid., p. 172.

33 Ibid.

3 Information and Planning

1 J.-J. Rousseau, *Du contract social* (Paris, 1996).

2 F. A. Hayek, 'Economics and Knowledge', *Economica* (1937), pp. 33–54.

3 Ibid., para. 3.30. This is taken from the online version available at www.econlib.org.

4 Ibid., para. 3.2.

5 Ibid.

6 Ibid.

7 Ibid., para. 3.3.

8 Ibid., para. 3.4.

9 Ibid., para. 3.6.

10 Ibid., para. 3.7, see also para. 3.32.

11 Ibid., para. 3.7.

12 Ibid., para. 3.8.

13 Ibid., para. 3.9.

14 See ibid., para. 3.15.

15 Ibid., para. 3.10.

16 Ibid., para. 3.13.

17 See H.-G. Gadamer, *Wahrheit und Methode: Grundzüge einer Philosophischen Hermeneutik* (Tübingen, 1975).

18 Hayek, 'Economics and Knowledge', para. 3.15.

19 Ibid., para. 3.16.

20 Ibid., para. 3.19.

21 See, for example, J. Habermas, *Theorie des kommunikativen Handelns*, vols I and II (Frankfurt, 1981), see also I. Berlin, 'Two Concepts of Liberty', in *Four Essays on Liberty* (Oxford, 1969).

22 Hayek, 'Economics and Knowledge', para. 3.20.

23 Ibid., para. 3.33, see also para. 3.36.

24 Ibid., para. 3.21.

25 Ibid., para. 3.25, see also para. 3.33.

26 Ibid., para. 3.29.

27 Ibid., para. 3.30.

28 Ibid., para. 3.31.

29 Ibid.

30 Berlin, 'Two Concepts of Liberty'; see also J. Habermas, *Theorie des kommunikativen Handelns*.

4 Keynes's General Theory

1 J. M. Keynes, *The General Theory of Employment, Interest and Money* [Cambridge, 1936] (London, 2008), pp. 25–6.

2 Ibid., pp. 26–7.

3 Ibid., p. 86.

4 Ibid., p. 240.

5 C. Black, *Franklin Delano Roosevelt: Champion of Freedom* (London, 2004), p. 285.

6 Keynes, *General Theory*, p. 109.

7 Ibid., p. 24.

8 Ibid., p. 114.

9 Ibid., p. 108.

10 Ibid., p. 242.

11 Ibid., p. 191.

12 Ibid., p. 242; see also p. 243.

13 Ibid., pp. 116–17.

14 Ibid., p. 14.

15 Ibid., p. 15.

16 Ibid., p. 117.

17 Ibid., pp. 17–18.

18 Ibid.

19 Ibid., p. 167.

20 Ibid., p. 169.

21 Ibid., p. 244.

22 F. A. Hayek, *The Road to Serfdom* (London, 1944), pp. 4–5, 9, 211.

23 See quote from F. D. Roosevelt, in Hayek, *Road to Serfdom*, p. 10; see also p. 203.

24 Hayek, *Road to Serfdom*, pp. 213–14.

25 Ibid., p. 126.

26 Ibid., p. 64.

27 See for example J. M. Keynes, *How to Pay for the War* (London, 1940).

28 Hayek, *Road to Serfdom*, pp. 3, 12–13.

29 Ibid., pp. 67–8.

30 Ibid., pp. 71, 74.

31 Ibid., pp. 117, 122.

32 Ibid., p. 73.

33 Ibid.

34 Ibid., p. 74.

5 Man is *Not* the Master of His Own Fate:
Misguided Socialist Idealism

1   See F. A. Hayek, *The Road to Serfdom* (London, 1944), Chapter Two, 'The Great Utopia'.

2   Ibid., p. 27.

3   E. Burke, *Thoughts and Details on Scarcity* [1800], available at Edmund Burke, Miscellaneous Writings, Liberty Fund, www.econlib.org, para. 4.4.43.

4   See also ibid., para. 4.4.48.

5   K. Marx, *Das Kapital: Kritik der politischen Ökonomie* [1872] (Cologne, 2000).

6   F. A. Hayek, *The Road to Serfdom* (London, 1944), pp. 20, 24.

7   See Burke, *Thoughts and Details on Scarcity*, para. 4.4.50–51.

8   Hayek, *Road to Serfdom*, p. 124.

9   Ibid., p. 26.

10 Burke, *Thoughts and Details on Scarcity*, para. 4.4.25, see also para. 4.4.41.

11 Hayek, *Road to Serfdom*, p. 124, see also pp. 125, 215.

12 Ibid., p. 21.

13 Ibid., p. 101.

14 Ibid., p. 127.

15 Ibid., pp. 22, 141.

16 Ibid., p. 118.

17 E. Burke, *Reflections on the Revolution in France, and Other Writings* (London, 1907).

18 Hayek, *Road to Serfdom*, pp. 13–14, 124.

19 J. M. Keynes, *The General Theory of Employment, Interest and Money* [Cambridge, 1936] (London, 2008), p. 240.

20 Ibid., p. 16.

21 T. Burczak, 'Hayekian Socialism, Post Critics', *Review of Social Economy*, LXVII/3 (September 2009), p. 390.

22 Burke, *Thoughts and Details on Scarcity*, para. 4.4.41.

23 Burczak, 'Hayekian Socialism', p. 390.

24 Ibid.

25 Marx, *Das Kapital*, chapters Five to Thirteen.

26 Keynes, *General Theory*, p. 243.

27 Ibid.

28 Friedrich Engels, *Herr Eugen Dührings Umwälzung der Wissenschaft* (Berlin, 1878), Chapter Two, Part 3, in Marx, Engels, *Werke* (Berlin), vol. XX, p. 9.

29 Kiesinger (CDU), in VDB, WP II, 5, p. 107A.

30 Schmid (SPD), in VDB, WP I, 10, p. 177C. Original: 'Es bedingt weiter, dass man die Schlüssel- und Grundstoffindustrien in Gemeineigentum überführt. Denn Demokratie als Bestimmung der Geschicke eines Volkes durch das Volk selbst gibt es nur dort, wo die Schalthebel der Wirtschaft nicht in Händen von Gruppen liegen, denen ihre wirtschaftliche Macht die Möglichkeit gibt, sich der demokratischen Kontrolle – jedenfalls einer wirksamen demokratischen Kontrolle – zu entziehen.'

31 Ollenhauer (SPD), in VDB, WP II, 4, p. 40B–C.

32 B. Bouvier, 'Erich Ollenhauer (1901–1963)', in *Deutsche Politiker, 1949–1969*, ed. T. Oppelland (Darmstadt, 1999), p. 196.

33 See W. Brandt, *Erinnerungen* (Frankfurt, 1989).

34 Deist (SPD), in VDB, WP II, 200, p. 11336D–11337A.

35 See G. W. Werner, *Einkommen für alle* (Cologne, 2007).

36 T. Burczak, 'Hayekian Socialism', p. 390.

37 Marx, *Das Kapital*.

38 K. Marx and F. Engels, *Das Kommunistische Manifest* [1848] (Hamburg, 1999).

39 M. Weitzmann, *The Share Economy* (Cambridge, MA, 1984), as quoted in Burczak, 'Hayekian Socialism', p. 391.

40 Burczak, 'Hayekian Socialism', pp. 391–2.

41 A. Agafonow, 'Toward a Positive Theory of Social Entrepreneurship: On Maximizing Versus Satisficing Value Capture', *Journal of Business Ethics*, CXXV/4 (2013).

42 M. Yunus, *Building Social Business: The New Kind of Capitalism that Serves Humanity's Most Pressing Needs* (New York, 2010).

43 Burczak, 'Hayekian Socialism', p. 392; for universal basic income see G. W. Werner, *Einkommen für alle* (Cologne, 2007); see also R. van der Veen and P. van Parijs, 'A Capitalist Road to Communism', *Basic Income Studies*, 1 (June 2006), pp. 1–23, and R. van der Veen and P. van Parijs, 'A Capitalist Road to Communism', *Theory and Society*,

xv/5 (1986), pp. 635–55. For universal capital grants see B. Ackermann, A. Alstott and P. van Parijs, *Redesigning Distribution* (London, 2006).

44 Werner, *Einkommen für alle*, p. 24.

45 Burczak, 'Hayekian Socialism', p. 392.

46 See Werner, *Einkommen für alle*, chapters Two and Three.

47 Keynes, *General Theory*, pp. 243–4.

48 Burke, *Thoughts and Details on Scarcity*, para. 4.4.72.

6 Liberal Polemic, or, the Threat of National Socialism

1 Quotation from Léon Jouhaux at the first Congress of the International Federation of Trade Unions in London, 1950, in Eccles (Con.) in *Hansard* (1950), 476, c. 1976, see also Boothby (Con.), in *Hansard* (1950), 476, c. 2119.

2 Eden (Con.), Minister for Dominion and Colonial Affairs, in *Hansard* (1939–40), 355, c. 755–62 [6 December 1939], reprinted A. Eden, *Freedom and Order* (London, 1947), p. 48.

3 F. A. Hayek, *The Road to Serfdom* (London, 1944), p. 173.

4 J. M. Keynes, *The General Theory of Employment, Interest and Money* [Cambridge, 1936] (London, 2008), pp. 27, 28.

5 Ibid., p. 28.

6 Ibid.

7 The Necessity of Planning

1 J. M. Keynes, *The General Theory of Employment, Interest and Money* [Cambridge, 1936] (London, 2008), p. 21.

2 Ibid., p. 61.

3 Ibid., p. 65.

4 Ibid., p. 66, see also, p. 77.

5 Ibid., p. 119, see also, p. 158.

6 Ibid., p. 244.

7 Ibid.

8 Ibid., p. 245.

9 Ibid.

10 Ibid., p. 61.

11 Leenhardt (PS), in JO, 1er Lég., 24 November 1949, pp. 6215III, 6218II, III.

12 Philip (PS), in JO, 1er Lég., 25 November 1949, p. 6304III.

13 Mollet (PS), in JO, 1er Lég., 25 November 1949, p. 6330II; see also Piette (PS), in JO, 3ème Lég., 5 July 1957, p. 3325I.

14 Ollenhauer (SPD), in VDB, WP II, 4, p. 40B–C.

15 Deist (SPD), in VDB, WP II, 200, p. 11336D–11337A.

16 Ollenhauer (SPD), in VDB, WP II, 4, p. 40B–C.

17 See W. Brandt, *Erinnerungen* (Frankfurt, 1989).

18 See T. C. Hörber, *The Origins of Energy and Environmental Policy in Europe: The Beginnings of a European Environmental Conscience* (London, 2013).

19 Hayek calls this 'the struggle of ideas', see F. A. Hayek, *The Road to Serfdom* (London, 1944), p. 11.

20 Ibid., p. 37.

21 Robson-Brown (Con.), in *Hansard* (1950), 478, c. 1812.

22 J. S. Mill, *Principles of Political Economy*, Book I, Chapter Two, para. 4, as quoted in Hayek, *Road to Serfdom*, pp. 116–17.

23 A. Smith quoted in Hayek, *Road to Serfdom*, p. 59.

24 E. Burke, *Thoughts and Details on Scarcity* [1800], available at Edmund Burke, Miscellaneous Writings, Liberty Fund, www.econlib.org, para. 4.4.17, see also para 4.4.113.

25 Hayek, *Road to Serfdom*, pp. 15, 210.

26 J. S. Mill, *Utilitarianism, Liberty and Representative Government* (London, 1910). See also R. Crisp, ed., *J. S. Mill: Utilitarianism* (Oxford, 1998), and J. Bentham, *An Introduction to the Principles of Morals and Legislation* (London, 1789).

27 Hayek, *Road to Serfdom*, pp. 59–60.

28 Ibid., p. 111.

29 Ibid., pp. 89, 107, 128–9.

30 Ibid., p. 34.

31 Ibid., p. 104.

32 Ibid., p. 79.

33 Adams (Lab.), in *Hansard* (1950), 476, c. 2025. See also, Silverman (Lab.), in *Hansard* (1950), 476, c. 2136, Morrison (Lab.), Lord President of the Council, in *Hansard* (1950), 478, c. 1741, and Blyton (Lab.), in *Hansard* (1950), 478, c. 1790.

34 Hayek, *Road to Serfdom*, pp. 148–9.

35 Ibid., p. 131.

36 Ibid., p. 128.

37 Ibid., pp. 131–2.

38 Ibid., p. 154.

39 Ibid., p. 138, see also more generally Chapter Ten, 'Why the Worst Get to the Top'.

40 Hayek, *Road to Serfdom*, p. 82, see also p. 150.

41 Ibid., p. 35 n. 1, referring to a memorandum written by Adam Smith in 1755; also pp. 112–13, 122. See also Burke, *Thoughts and Details on Scarcity*, para. 4.4.113.

8 Liberty and Totalitarianism

1   F. A. Hayek, *The Road to Serfdom* (London, 1944), pp. 6, 27–30, 60, 90, 172.

2   Ibid., p. 92.

3   K. Marx and F. Engels, *Das Kommunistische Manifest* [1848] (Hamburg, 1999).

4   I. Berlin, 'Two Concepts of Liberty', in *Four Essays on Liberty* (Oxford, 1969), p. 127.

5   Hayek, *Road to Serfdom*, pp. 92–3.

6   J. M. Keynes, *The General Theory of Employment, Interest and Money* [Cambridge, 1936] (London, 2008), p. 190.

7   Hayek, *Road to Serfdom*, p. 61, see also pp. 94, 154.

8   Ibid., p. 61.

9   Ibid., pp. 62–3.

10 Ibid., pp. 166–7, 169, 211.

11 Ibid., pp. 89, 95, 150.

12 Berlin, 'Two Concepts of Liberty', p. 163.

13 Hayek, *Road to Serfdom*, pp. 143–4.

14 Ibid., pp. 157–8.

15 Berlin, 'Two Concepts of Liberty', p. 148.

16 Hayek, *Road to Serfdom*, p. 151.

17 Ibid., pp. 153–4. See also D. C. Coyle, 'The Twilight of National Planning', *Harper's Magazine* (October 1935), p. 558, as quoted in Hayek, *Road to Serfdom*, p. 130.

18 Hayek, *Road to Serfdom*, p. 150.

19 Ibid., pp. 61–2.

20 Ibid., p. 152.

21 Ibid., pp. 222–3.

22 N. Henderson, *Failure of a Mission: Berlin, 1937–1939* (London, 1940), p. vii.

23 Attlee (Lab.), Prime Minister, in *Hansard* (1950), 478, c. 953.

24 Wehner (SPD), in VDB, WP I, 85, p. 3188B. Original: 'Das kommunistische System bedeutet Vernichtung der Menschenrechte, Versklavung der arbeitenden Menschen, Verewigung von Hunger, Elend und

Ausbeutung. Die kommunistischen Machthaber sind die wahren Kriegshetzer gegen das eigene Volk. (Stürmischer Beifall von der SPD bis zur BP.)'. See also Adenauer (CDU), Chancellor, in VDB, WP I, 98, p. 3565C, Schmid (SPD), in VDB, WP II 71, p. 3820A, and P. Merseburger, 'Kurt Schumacher (1895–1952)', in *Deutsche Politiker, 1949–1969*, ed. T. Oppelland (Darmstadt, 1999), p. 108.

25 See Hayek, *Road to Serfdom*, p. 42.

26 Ibid., pp. 25, 141.

27 See E. Laclau and C. Mouffe, *Hegemony and Socialist Strategy* (London, 1985).

28 See, for example, R. Taylor, *The TUC: From the General Strike to New Unionism* (Basingstoke, 2000).

29 Keynes, *General Theory*, p. 244.

30 Burke, *Thoughts and Details on Scarcity*, para. 4.4.25.

31 Keynes, *General Theory*, p. 245.

32 Ibid., p. 79.

33 Ibid., p. 158.

34 See T. Hobbes, *Leviathan* (Oxford, 1996), and J. Locke, *Two Treatises of Government* (Cambridge, 1960). See also J.-J. Rousseau, *Du contrat social* (Paris 1996), and Burke, *Thoughts and Details on Scarcity*, para. 4.4.39; also para. 4.4.113.

35 Burke, *Thoughts and Details on Scarcity*, para. 4.4.115.

36 Hayek, *Road to Serfdom*, p. 17.

37 Ibid., p. 37.

38 Ibid., p. 38.

9 International Organizations and European Integration

1 F. A. Hayek, *The Road to Serfdom* (London, 1944), p. 40.

2 Ibid., p. 226.

3 J. Monnet, 'Algiers Memorandum', in *Building European Union: A Documentary History and Analysis*, ed. T. Salmon and W. Nicoll (Manchester, 1997), Document 7, pp. 21–2.

4 Hayek, *Road to Serfdom*, pp. 227, 238.

5 As used ibid., p. 227.

6 Ibid., p. 228.

7 Ibid., p. 236.

8 See T. C. Hörber, *The Foundations of Europe: European Integration Ideas in France, Germany and Britain in the 1950s* (Wiesbaden, 2006), and T. C. Hörber, *A Converging Post-war European Discourse: War*

Experience, Changing Security Concepts, and Research and Education (Lanham, MD, 2014). In both books see the chapters on Britain/ National Security, Economic Security and War Experience.

9 Hayek, *Road to Serfdom*, p. 239.

10 See S. George, *An Awkward Partner: Britain in the European Community* (Oxford, 1998).

11 Hayek, *Road to Serfdom*, p. 241.

12 Ibid., p. 242.

13 Monnet, 'Algiers Memorandum', p. 21.

14 Hayek, *Road to Serfdom*, p. 243.

15 See Teitgen (MRP), in JO, 2ème Lég., 22 December 1954, p. 6750II. See also Gozard (PS), in JO, 3ème Lég., 16 January 1957, p. 78II.

16 Teitgen (MRP), in JO, 2ème Lég., 22 December 1954, p. 6750II.

17 Maurice Faure (RRS), in JO, 2ème Lég., 7 December 1951, p. 8956II.

18 Schuman (MRP), Foreign Minister, in JO, 1er Lég., 2 December 1948, p. 7345II.

19 Mollet (PS), in JO, 1er Lég., 25 November 1949, p. 6330III.

20 Bonnefous (UDSR), President of the Committee for Foreign Policy, in JO, 1er Lég., 25 July 1950, p. 5917I.

21 'The Schuman Declaration', in A. G. Harryman and J. van der Harst, *Documents on European Union* (Basingstoke, 1997), Document II, pp. 61–3.

22 J. M. Keynes, *The General Theory of Employment, Interest and Money* [Cambridge, 1936] (London, 2008), p. 243.

23 There are many published criticisms of the EU's management of the financial crisis; see for example G. Soros, *The Tragedy of the European Union: Disintegration or Revival?* (New York, 2014).

24 Keynes, *General Theory*, p. 68.

25 Ibid., p. 72.

26 Ibid., p. 246.

27 For the most seminal work for the economic arguments for European integration see A. S. Milward, *The European Rescue of the Nation-state* (London, 2000). See also A. S. Milward, *The Reconstruction of Western Europe, 1945–51* (London, 1984).

28 F. A. Hayek, 'Economics and Knowledge', *Economica* (1937), available at www.econlib.org, accessed 20 July 2015, para. 3.35.

29 Keynes, *General Theory*, p. 110.

30 Ibid., p. 112.

31 Ibid., p. 86.

32 Ibid., p. 75.

33 Ibid., p. 68.

34 Ibid.

35 Ibid., p. 76.

36 Ibid., p. 156.

37 Ibid., p. 157.

38 Ibid., p. 159.

39 Ibid., p. 157.

40 E. Burke, *Thoughts and Details on Scarcity* [1800], available at Edmund Burke, Miscellaneous Writings, Liberty Fund, www.econlib.org, para. 4.4.72.

41 Soros, *Tragedy of the European Union*, p. 158.

42 Ibid., p. 57.

43 Hellwig (CDU/CSU), in VDB, WP II, 200, p. 11361B.

Conclusion

1 I. Berlin, 'Two Concepts of Liberty', in *Four Essays on Liberty* (Oxford, 1969), p. 169.

2 J. M. Keynes, *The General Theory of Employment, Interest and Money* [Cambridge, 1936] (London, 2008), p. 242.

3 See T. C. Hörber, 'European Space Policy', *Space Policy*, XXVIII/2 (May 2012). See also T. C. Hörber and P. Stephenson, eds, *European Space Policy: European Integration and the Final Frontier* (London, 2015).

4 See A. Agafonow, C. Donaldson and T. C. Hörber, eds, 'Unveiling the Economic Rationale behind the Social Business Model', *Social Business*, V/1 (Spring 2015).

5 T. C. Hörber and P. Barnes, eds, *Sustainability Discourse in the European Union: Reconciliation of Energy and Environmental Policies* (London, 2013).

6 World Commission on Environment and Development (UN WCED) (1987), *Our Common Future, the 'Brundtland Report'* (BR), Annex to General Assembly Document A/42/427: Development and International Co-operation: Environment, delivered 2 August 1987, United Nations, New York, available at www.un-documents.net, accessed 19 October 2016.

7 E. Burke, *Thoughts and Details on Scarcity* [1800], available at Edmund Burke, Miscellaneous Writings, Liberty Fund, www.econlib.org, para. 4.4.4.

8 Keynes, *General Theory*, pp. 155, 242.

9   For the definition of sustainable development as 'social, environmental
    and economic' see 'Report of the World Commission on Environment
    and Development: Our Common Future' (1987) [Brundtland
    Report], at www.un-documents.net/our-common-future.pdf.

10 F. A. Hayek, *The Road to Serfdom* (London, 1944), p. 244.

11 Ibid., p. 246.

12 Ibid., p. 43.

13 Ibid., p. 106.

14 Ibid., p. 105.

15 Keynes, *General Theory*, p. 241.

16 Philip (PS), in JO, 1er Lég., 25 November 1949, p. 6304III.

17 Keynes, *General Theory*, p. 245.

18 Wahl (CDU), in VDB, WP I, 183, p. 7724A. Original: 'dass die Kriege der
    Vergangenheit zu einem wesentlichen Teil Wirtschaftskriege gewesen
    sind. Dieser Gedanke führt zwangsläufig zu dem Versuch, Mittel und
    Wege zu finden, um den Konkurrenzkampf der Volkswirtschaften zu
    beseitigen.'

19 See Teitgen (MRP), in JO, 2ème Lég., 22 December 1954, p. 6750II.
    See also Gozard (PS), in JO, 3ème Lég., 16 January 1957, p. 78II.

20 Keynes, *General Theory*, p. 246.

21 Ibid., p. 247.

22 F. A. Hayek, 'Economics and Knowledge', *Economica* (1937), available
    at www.econlib.org, accessed 10 July 2015, para. 3.5.

23 Ibid., para. 3.36.

24 Ibid., para. 3.39.

25 Ibid.

Bibliography

Ackermann, B., A. Alstott and P. Van Parijs, *Redesigning Distribution* (London, 2006)

Addleson, M., *Equilibrium versus Understanding: Towards the Restoration of Economics as Social Theory* (London, 1995)

Agafonow, A., 'Toward a Positive Theory of Social Entrepreneurship: On Maximizing versus Satisficing Value Capture', *Journal of Business Ethics*, CXXV/4 (2013)

Azariadis, C., and J. Stiglitz, 'Implicit Contract and Fixed-price Equilibria', in *New Keynesian Economics*, vol. II, ed. N. G. Mankiw and D. Romer (Cambridge, MA, 1991)

——, 'Implicit Contract and Fixed-price Equilibria', *Quarterly Journal of Economics*, 98, supplement (1983), pp. 1–22

Bailey, M. N., 'Wages and Employment Under Uncertain Demand', *Review of Economic Studies*, XLI (1974), pp. 37–50

Bentham, J., *An Introduction to the Principles of Morals and Legislation* (London, 1789)

Berlin, I., 'Two Concepts of Liberty', in *Four Essays on Liberty* (Oxford, 1969)

Black, C., *Franklin Delano Roosevelt: Champion of Freedom* (London, 2004)

Boettke, P., *Calculation and Coordination* (London, 2001)

——, ed., *Elgar Companion to Austrian Economics* (Aldershot, 1994)

——, 'Review of Joseph Stiglitz's *Whither Socialism?*', *Journal of Economic Literature*, XXXIV (1996), pp. 189–91

Bouvier, B., 'Erich Ollenhauer (1901–1963)', in *Deutsche Politiker, 1949–1969*, ed. T. Oppeland (Darmstadt, 1999), pp. 187–97

Bowles, S., and H. Gintis, 'The Revenge of Homo Economicus: Contested Exchange and Revival of Political Economy', *Journal of Economic Perspectives*, VII/1 (1993), pp. 83–102

Brandt, W., *Erinnerungen* (Frankfurt, 1989)

Burczak, T., 'Hayekian Socialism, Post Critics', *Review of Social Economy*,
    LXVII/3 (September 2009), pp. 389–94

—, *Socialism after Hayek* (Ann Arbor, MI, 2006)

Burke, E., *Reflections on the Revolution in France, and Other Writings*
    (Oxford, 1907)

—, *A Philosophical Enquiry into Sublime and Beautiful* (London, 2008)

—, *Thoughts and Details on Scarcity* (London, 1800)

—, *Thoughts and Details on Scarcity* [1800], available at Edmund Burke,
    Miscellaneous Writings, Liberty Fund, www.econlib.org

Burns, J. H., and H.L.A. Hart, eds, *Jeremy Bentham: An Introduction to the*
    Principles of Morals and Legislation (Oxford, 1996)

Caldwell, B., 'Hayek and Socialism', *Journal of Economic Literature*, XXXV
    (1997), pp. 1856–90

Coyle, D. C., 'The Twilight of National Planning', *Harper's Magazine*
    (October 1935)

Crisp, R., ed., *J. S. Mill: Utilitarianism* (Oxford, 1998)

Dasgupta, P., *An Inquiry into Well-being and Destruction* (Oxford, 1993)

de Gaulle, C., *Mémoires d'espoir* (Paris, 1999)

Dobb, M., *Political Economy and Capitalism* (New York, 1945)

Eastman, M., *The Reader's Digest* (July 1941)

Eden, A., *Freedom and Order* (London, 1947)

Ellerman, D., *Property and Contract in Economics* (Oxford, 1992)

Farrant, A., 'Knowledge and Incentives: Socialism after Hayek?', *Review*
    of Social Economy, LXVII/3 (September 2009)

Frank, J., *Law and Modern Mind* (Gloucester, MA, 1930)

Gadamer H.-G., 'Die Antropologische Grundlage der Freiheit des
    Menschen', in *Das Erbe Europas* (Frankfurt, 1989)

—, 'Die Aufgabe der Philosopie', in *Das Erbe Europas* (Frankfurt, 1989)

—, 'Die Grenzen des Experten', in *Das Erbe Europas* (Frankfurt, 1989)

—, 'Die Vielfalt Europas Erbe und Zukunft', in *Das Erbe Europas*
    (Frankfurt, 1989)

—, *Hermeneutics, Religion, and Ethics*, trans. J. Weinheimer (New Haven,
    CT, 1999)

—, *Wahrheit und Methode: Grundzüge einer Philosophischen Hermeneutik*,
    4th edn (Tübingen, 1975)

George, S., *An Awkward Partner: Britain in the European Community*
    (Oxford, 1998)

Gordon, D. F., 'A Neoclassical Theory of Keynesian Unemployment',
    Economic Enquiry, XII (1974), pp. 431–59

Gray, J., and G. W. Smith, eds, *J. S. Mill: On Liberty* (London, 1991)

Habermas, J., *Theorie des kommunikativen Handelns*, vols I and II (Frankfurt, 1981)

Hansard, vols 355 (1939), 476 (1950), 478 (1950)

Harryman, A. G., and J. van der Harst, *Documents on European Union* (Basingstoke, 1997)

Hayek, F. A., 'Competition as a Discovery Procedure', in *New Studies in Philosophy, Politics, Economics and the History of Ideas* (Chicago, IL, 1978), pp. 179–90

——, *The Construction of Liberty* (London, 1960)

——, 'Economics and Knowledge', *Economica* (1937), pp. 33–54

——, *Individualism and Economic Order* (Chicago, IL, 1948)

——, *Law, Legislation and Liberty*, vol. I: *Rules and Order* (Chicago, IL, 1973)

——, 'The Meaning of Competition', in *Individualism and Economic Order* (London, 1949), pp. 92–106

——, *New Studies in Philosophy, Politics, Economics and the History of Ideas* (Chicago, IL, 1978)

——, *The Political Order of a Free People* (Chicago, IL, 1979)

——, *The Road to Serfdom* (London, 1944)

——, 'The Use of Knowledge in Society', *American Economic Review*, XXXV (1945), pp. 519–30

Henderson, N., *Failure of a Mission: Berlin, 1937–1939* (London, 1940)

Hirshleifer, J., and J. G. Riley, *The Analytics of Uncertainty and Information* (Cambridge, 1993)

Hobbes, T., *Leviathan* (Oxford, 1996)

Hörber, T. C., *A Converging Post-war European Discourse: War Experience, Changing Security Concepts, and Research and Education* (Lanham, MD, 2014)

——, 'European Space Policy', *Space Policy*, XXVIII/2 (May 2012)

——, *The Foundations of Europe: European Integration Ideas in France, Germany and Britain in the 1950s* (Wiesbaden, 2006)

——, *The Origins of Energy and Environmental Policy in Europe: The Beginnings of a European Environmental Conscience* (London, 2013)

Hörber, T. C., and P. Stephenson, eds, *European Space Policy: European Integration and the Final Frontier* (London, 2015)

Hörber, T. C., and P. Barnes, eds, *Sustainability Discourse in the European Union: Reconciliation of Energy and Environmental Policies* (London, 2013)

Ikeda, S., *Dynamics of the Mixed Economy* (London, 1996)

Keynes, J. M., *The Economic Consequences of the Peace* (New York, 1919)

—, *The General Theory of Employment, Interest and Money* [Cambridge, 1936] (London, 2008)

—, *How to Pay for the War* (London, 1940)

Kirzner, I. M., *Competition and Entrepreneurship* (Chicago, IL, 1973)

—, 'Entrepreneurial Discovery and the Competitive Market Process: An Austrian Approach', *Journal of Economic Literature*, XXXV (1997), pp. 60–85

—, 'Market Process Theory: In Defence of the Austrian Middle Ground', in *The Meaning of Market Process: Essays in the Development of Modern Austrian Economics* (London, 1992), pp. 3–37

—, 'The Meaning of Market Process', in *The Meaning of Market Process: Essays in the Development of Modern Austrian Economics* (London, 1992), pp. 38–54

—, ed., *Method, Process and Austrian Economics: Essays in Honor of Ludwig von Mises* (Lexington, MA, 1982)

Kreps, O. M., 'Static Choice in the Presence of Unforeseen Contingencies', in *Economic Analysis of Markets and Games: Essays in Honor of Frank Hahn*, ed. P. Dasgupta et al. (Cambridge, MA, 1992), pp. 258–81

Lachmann, L. M., 'Austrian Economics: A Hermeneutic Approach', in *Economics and Hermeneutics*, ed. D. Lavoie (London, 1990), pp. 134–46

—, *Capital, Expectations, and the Market Process: Essays on the Theory of the Market Economy* (Kansas City, KS, 1977)

—, 'From Mises to Shackles: An Essay in Austrian Economics and the Kaleidic Society', *Journal of Economic Literature*, XIV (1976), pp. 54–62

—, *The Market as an Economic Process* (Oxford, 1986)

Laclau, E., and C. Mouffe, *Hegemony and Socialist Strategy* (London, 1985)

Lavoie, D., ed., *Economics and Hermeneutics* (London, 1990)

—, 'The Interpretative Turn', in *Elgar Companion to Austrian Economics*, ed. P. Boettke (Aldershot, 1994), pp. 54–62

Lawson, T., *Economics and Reality* (London, 1997)

Levi, I., *Hard Choices: Decision-making under Unresolved Conflict* (Cambridge, 1986)

—, 'The Paradoxes of Allais and Ellsberg', *Economics and Philosophy*, II (1986), pp. 23–53

Lindbeck, A., 'New Keynesianism and Aggregate Economic Activity', *Economic Journal*, CVIII (1998), pp. 167–80

Locke, J., *Two Treatises of Government* (Cambridge, 1960)

Madan, D. P., and J. C. Owings, 'Decision Theory with Complex Uncertainties', *Synthese*, LXXV (1988), pp. 25–44

Mäki, U., 'Practical Syllogism, Entrepreneurship and the Invisible Hand: A Critique of the Analytic Hermeneutics of G. H von Wright', in *Economics and Hermeneutics*, ed. D. Lavoie (London, 1990), pp. 149–76

Marglin, S., 'What Do Bosses Do? The Origins and Functions of Hierarchy in Capitalist Production', *Review of Radical Political Economy*, VI (1974), pp. 60–112

Marx, K., *Das Kapital: Kritik der politischen Ökonomie* [1872] (Cologne, 2000)

——, and F. Engels, *Das Kommunistische Manifest* [1848] (Hamburg, 1999)

Merriam, C. E., 'Review of Hayek's *Road to Serfdom*', *American Journal of Sociology*, L/3 (1944), pp. 233–5

——, 'Review of Wooton's *Freedom Under Planning* and Finer's *Road to Reaction*', *American Political Science Review*, XL/1 (1946), pp. 133–6

Merseburger, P., 'Kurt Schumacher (1895–1952)', in *Deutsche Politiker, 1949–1969*, ed. T. Oppelland (Darmstadt, 1999)

Mill, J. S., *Utilitarianism, Liberty and Representative Government* (London, 1910)

Milward, A. S., *The European Rescue of the Nation-state* (London, 2000)

——, *The Reconstruction of Western Europe, 1945–51* (London, 1984)

Mises, L., *Human Action* (New Haven, CT, 1949)

Monnet, J., 'Algiers Memorandum (August 1943)', in *Building European Union: A Documentary History and Analysis*, ed. T. Salmon and W. Nicoll (Manchester, 1997), document 7, pp. 21–2

Musgrave, A., '"Unreal Assumptions" in Economic Theory: The F-twist Untwisted', *Kyklos*, XXXIV (1981), pp. 377–87

O'Driscoll, G. P., and M. J. Rizzo, *The Economics of Time and Ignorance* (Oxford, 1985)

Oppelland, T., ed., *Deutsche Politiker, 1949–1969* (Darmstadt, 1999)

Popper, K. R., *A World of Propensities* (Bristol, 1990)

Prychitko, D. L., 'Ludwig Lachmann and the Interpretative Turn in Economics: A Critical Enquiry into the Hermeneutics of the Plan', *Advances in Austrian Economics*, I (1994), pp. 303–19

'Report of the World Commission on Environment and Development: Our Common Future' (1987) [aka Brundtland Report], available at www.un-documents.net/our-common-future.pdf

Resnick, S., and R. Wolff, *Knowledge and Class* (Chicago, IL, 1987)

Robbins, L., 'Hayek on Liberty', *Economica*, XXVIII (1961), pp. 66–81

Rosen, S., 'Austrian and Neoclassical Economics: Any Gains from Trade?', *Journal of Economic Perspectives*, XXI (1997), pp. 139–52

Rousseau, J.-J., *Du contrat social* (Paris, 1996)

Runde J., 'Assessing Causal Economic Explanations', in *Oxford Economic Papers*, L (1998), pp. 151–72

——, 'Bringing Social Structure Back into Economics: On Critical Realism and Hayek's Scientism Essay', *Review of Austrian Economics*, XIV (2001), pp. 5–24

——, 'Idealisation, Abstraction and Economic Theory', in *Markets, Unemployment and Economic Theory: Essays in Honor of Geoff Harcourt*, ed. P. Arestis. G. Palma and M. Sawyer (London, 1996), vol. II, pp. 16–29

——, 'Information, Knowledge and Agency: The Information Theoretic Approach and the Austrians', *Review of Social Economy*, LX/2 (June 2002), pp. 183–208

——, 'On Popper, Probabilities and Propensities', *Review of Social Economy*, 54 (1996), pp. 465–85

Salmon, T., and W. Nicoll, eds, *Building European Union: A Documentary History and Analysis* (Manchester, 1997)

'The Schuman Declaration', in *Documents on European Union*, ed. A. G. Harryman and J. van der Harst (Basingstoke, 1997), document 11, pp. 61–3

Searle, J. R., *The Construction of Social Reality* (Harmondsworth, 1995)

Shackle, G., *Epistemics and Economics: A Critique of Economic Doctrine* (Cambridge, 1972)

Smith, A., *An Inquiry into the Nature and Causes of the Wealth of Nations* [1776] (Oxford, 1976)

——, *An Inquiry into the Nature and Causes of the Wealth of Nations* [1776] (Oxford, 1979)

——, *An Inquiry into the Nature and Causes of the Wealth of Nations* [1776] (Oxford, 1993)

Soros, G., *The Tragedy of the European Union: Disintegration or Revival?* (New York, 2014)

Stigler, G., *Memoirs of an Unregulated Economist* (New York, 1988)

Stiglitz, J., 'The Causes and Consequences of the Dependence of Quality on Price', *Journal of Economic Literature*, 25 (1987), pp. 1–48

——, 'Information and Economic Analysis: A Perspective', in Supplements to the *Economic Journal*, 95 (1985), pp. 21–41

——, *Whither Socialism?* (Cambridge, MA, 1994)

Sullivan, S., 'Signifying Nothing: A Review Essay of Joseph Stiglitz, *Whither Socialism?*', *Advances in Austrian Economics*, III (1996), pp. 183–9

Taylor, R., *The TUC: From the General Strike to New Unionism* (Basingstoke, 2000)

Thomsen, E. F., *Prices and Knowledge: A Market-Process Perspective* (London, 1992)

Vaughn, K. I., *Austrian Economics in America: The Migration of a Tradition* (Cambridge, 1994)

Veen, R. van der, and P. Van Parijs, 'A Capitalist Road to Communism', *Theory and Society*, XV/5 (1986), pp. 635–55

Verhandlungen des Deutschen Bundestages, 1.-3. Wahlperiode (WP) (Bonn, 1949–61)

——, 'A Capitalist Road to Communism', *Basic Income Studies*, I (June 2006), pp. 1–23

Weitzmann, M., *The Share Economy* (Cambridge, MA, 1984)

Werner, G. W., *Einkommen für alle* (Cologne, 2007)

World Commission on Environment and Development (UN WCED) (1987), *Our Common Future, the 'Brundtland Report'* (BR), Annex to General Assembly Document A/42/427: Development and International Co-operation: Environment, delivered 2 August 1987, United Nations, New York, available at www.un-documents.net, accessed 19 October 2016

Yunus, M., *Building Social Business: The New Kind of Capitalism that Serves Humanity's Most Pressing Needs* (New York, 2010)

Acknowledgements

It has to be admitted that the author of this book is not an economist. My interest in economic theory came originally from the study of political theory and history at Trinity Hall, Cambridge. Teaching at a business school, many years later, necessitated the adaptation of those interests and led, almost inevitably, to economic theory. Luckily, I was not alone in this learning process. I would like to thank my students, who have accompanied me on this passage of economic, political and social understanding, which has led to this book. I would also like to express my gratitude to Professor Albrecht Sonntag at ESSCA School of Management for letting me run with a research and publication project of uncertain outcome, and to Dr Amanar Akhabbar, who gave me food for economic thought. Finally, I would like to thank Mr Richard Dunn, BA (Econ), MA, MPhil (Cantab), who has proofread – although he will not like the term – all my works. For a non-native speaker such as myself, such a service is worth its weight in gold. It has helped me enormously on the competitive path of an academic career. For that reason and for our long friendship, which has taken me often back to Cambridge, I would like to dedicate this book to him.

Index

abolition of money 89–90
Australian school of economics 31
authoritarianism 9, 30–31, 45, 52,
    60, 65, 70–71, 73
    and war 93–4

basic income 66–8
Bretton Woods 10
Brexit 106
British Labour Party 71, 94, 96
British parliamentary model 30
Brundtland report 120
Burczak, Theodore 15
Burke, Edmund 10, 17–18, 20–21,
    56, 58, 94, 101, 120

corruption 30, 80, 84, 90, 100
Cambridge arrogance 12
change, acceptance of 115–16
Chicago economists 11
child labour 10
Churchill, Winston 85
citizens and land, link between
    120–21
Cold War 9, 30, 70–71
Communism 88, 90, 94–5
    cleavage with socialism 95–7
Communist Manifesto 88

competitive advantage 16
crisis 63
    1970s 82
    of 2008 109–10, 124
    Greece 24
criticism reaction 12–13, 25

data, concept of objective and
    subjective 39–40, 42
'deficit spending' policy 44–5
'democratic deficit' 104
destination of economics as a
    discipline 13–14
division of labour 27
dominant social forces, the interest
    of 75

economic immigration 11
economic motive 89
economic objectives 25
economic tools, use of 50
economic war 126
employment 12, 33, 43–7, 51–3,
    60–64, 78–9, 99–100
    as a commodity 33, 58, 98, 113
    'involuntary employment' 33,
    49–50, 77
Engels, Friedrich 88

entrepreneurial activity 120
ethics 48, 51, 80, 92
European Coal and Steel
    Community 105–6
European Union 16, 122–3
    budget 111
    enlargement 106–7
    integration 86, 105

federalism 106
First World War 19, 71, 103
freedom 10–11, 22–3, 80, 92
    civil 21, 31, 55–9, 70
    economic 17, 27, 75
    political 11
French Socialist Party 96
'functionless investor' 48, 51–2,
    119

Gadamer, Hans-Georg 42
theory of hermeneutics 39
Godesberg programme, 63, 81, 96
Great Depression, the 8, 19, 33, 44,
    74–6, 89, 119

happiness, pursuit of 22
Hayek, Friedrich August von
    The Road to Serfdom 9, 12

imperfection of human nature 29
individual decision 32, 38–9, 41,
    122
    see also knowledge of individual
        actor
individualism 97–8
Industrial Revolution 20
inequality 20–21, 57, 75, 124
interest rate 45–50, 78, 115–16
    in the Eurozone 113

international institutions 10, 103
Iron and Steel Act of the Labour
    government 83

Keynes, John Maynard
    *General Theory of Employment,
        Interest and Money* 8, 12
knowledge 28, 124, 129
    communication 128
    division of 41
    of individual actor 18, 37, 40,
        42, 112

League of Nations 10, 103
loyalty to the nation 71

market
    imperfection 19, 69
    transparency 18
Marx, Karl 7–8, 31, 74
    alienation 61–2, 68
minimum income 64
Mollet, Guy 107
Monnet, Jean 103–6

national sovereignty 105
nationalization of industries 81
Nazi 9, 16, 31, 86

Organisation for European
    Economic Co-operation 105
ownership 85–6

parliament democracy, the
    preservation of 54
payment, other means of 24
politics in post-war period 71–2
poverty 44–5, 58–60, 68
power 85–6

power of ideas, the 127
price setting 18, 26–7, 42, 59, 102
profit 10, 22, 28–9, 51, 100
   -driven decision 32
   maximization 11, 18, 26
   non-profit 24, 65
   rationale 65

quantitative easing 47
quantitative versus qualitative
   economics 13–15, 129–30

regulation of the financial sector 119
Roosevelt, Franklin Delano
   'New Deal' policy 12, 35, 45,
   52–3, 127–8
Rousseau, Jean-Jacques
   The Social Contract 36

Schuman declaration 85, 107
Second World War 8–11, 16, 19, 44,
   70
self-fulfilling prophecy 38
Smith, Adam 7–8, 10, 16, 83
   invisible hand 18, 27
Social Democratic Party 63, 81, 96

social injustice *see* inequality
Soros, George
   'double distortion' 117
Social theory 7, 25, 48, 68
speculation 47–8, 117
supply, exclusive consideration of
   74, 77
sustainability 11, 80, 118–21

taxation 20, 23–4, 52, 108
'the impersonal character of the
   process' 123
'the abandoned road' 19
'too big to fail' 124
trade policies, aggressive 126–7

Union of Soviet Socialist Republics
   62, 93–4
uncertainty *see* knowledge
utilitarianism 84
utopia, the threat of 29–30

wages 23–4, 33, 44, 59, 75, 77
   money-wage 33, 49–51
Weimar Republic 11, 44
welfare state, creation 29–30